SEPARATION
Journal of a Marriage

by Eve Baguedor

SIMON AND SCHUSTER

NEW YORK

FIRST PRINTING
SBN 671–21208–7
Library of Congress Catalog Card Number: 72–83927
Designed by Irving Perkins
Manufactured in the United States of America
By H. Wolff Book Mfg. Co., Inc., New York, N.Y.

Contents

5

According to Government statistics, 600,000 couples separate each year.

—*The New York Times*

. . . all this present reality of yours is fated to seem a mere illusion to you tomorrow.

—Pirandello

Asunder

An event has happened, upon which it is difficult
to speak, and impossible to be silent.
—EDMUND BURKE

I T I S Hank's forty-ninth birthday and we are in the fullness
of our sullen, retaliatory silence. I do not yet know, do not
wish to know, that this impasse is to be our last; that in six
weeks, Hank will walk out. I choose to hold tight to custom
by giving a small dinner party for Hank and a few close
friends. The table is festive with Royal Blue Copenhagen
and a centerpiece of daffodils and white stock. I serve Hank's
unchanging favorite: beef, slightly rare, surrounded by tiny
glazed carrots and white onions. Hank, as usual, selects the
wine: a bottle of white Burgundy. But neither the good food
nor the fine wine can make the atmosphere "rise." Before
the coffee, I observe the birthday ceremoniously, carrying in
a cupcake with one lighted candle. Good feeling is stirred
for an instant, but is snuffed out for lack of spontaneity.
There is something far too wrong.

I am too late for forms. The tensions between us are at

9

the flood, and neither the bonds of habit nor of mutuality can hold.

Later that night, Hank is amorous, as he is when drinking. My own inner wires are too taut and tangled to respond freely, easily, but I go along. Suddenly, in the midst of love-making, Hank is dizzy and rushes from the bed to the bathroom. I hear him being sick—violently sick. I go in to hold his head, to help him freshen up. I clean the bathroom floor. Afterward, he is pale and shaken and tells me over and over: "Nobody has ever loved me. Nobody has ever loved me." But he assures me that I am "a nice girl, a really nice girl," and falls asleep. In those minutes, as I watch him—this man I have lived with for twenty years—I am sad and compassionate, and ill with his despair and my own guilt.

A month later, Hank serves notice: he is deciding whether he will stay or leave. He will make up his mind in the next few weeks, he tells me, adding: "I am a proud and stubborn man. Once I walk out that door, I will not come back."

In two more weeks, he announces his decision: he is leaving. We are sitting on the lawn swing when Hank tells me. Erika and Jill, sixteen, our unalike twins, are in the house—out of earshot. This is the confrontation between us, no less angry than any confrontation of blacks against whites, of students against authority, although we are outwardly composed, our voices held down. We hide behind our eyes, behind whatever words our mouths can form. I nod in response to Hank's pronouncement, reply bodily with a shrug of one shoulder. I am expending all my energy in remaining calm. I say nothing. I look down at the seat of the swing and think: "This needs a fresh coat of paint."

Now we look directly at each other, too defiant to hide, too stiff to talk. Hank appears composed, his blue eyes cold, his jaw tensed. My face, I know, is already strained. We are two solid blocks of resentment, of justification, each to ourselves. There is *no* breakdown of communication. Through the silence, Hank is signaling his urgency to get out, and I, my search for relief. I say soundlessly: "Go! Go, if you are going. I want you to go!"

The escape hatch is opening. We are opening it with the magic word "out."

Out is a great open space with relief from pain, with the possibility of an intriguing new life, with a new "me" in the offing for each of us. But I am afraid as I see it happening. I am at the center of a great space that starts in my mind, envelops me, but does not reach out to touch the real world.

I could not have made a rapprochement then if I had tried; certainly not by the route I'd gone with Hank thousands of times—my small offerings of conciliation, humor, appeasement. The moment calls for a great explosion of anger, even physical violence, but we are not practiced at, perhaps not capable of, this.

It is far more characteristic of us, behaved to the last, that we go on living together in the house for a week after Hank announces he will leave. We address each other with inviolable politeness, mocking old habits:

"Good morning. Would you like peaches on your cornflakes?" I ask him.
"Good night. Would you like me to turn down the air conditioner?" he asks me.

On one of these last, disembodied evenings, Hank suggests that we ride out into the country and talk once more. We do not come face to face; he is attending to the driving and

I am hypnotized by the road. We are wary of each other, but I think I must say something. Always, in a silence, I think I must say something.

"Part of me is resentful that you are leaving," I tell Hank; "part of me wishes you luck—if you think you can find a better new life for yourself." I am *not* sarcastic. I am still partly the wife, still in the habit of helping Hank to find self-realization, some peace of mind.

I also say, "I will not sabotage you with the children."

Hank nods. "I know you won't."

We are—more fools, both of us!—sincere, fatuous, and uninformed.

That same evening Hank tells Erika and Jill that he is going. Jill runs to her room and sobs behind a closed door. Erika cries openly. Afterward, both girls walk through the house subdued and hushed, as though in the aftermath of a death.

When Hank moves out, I am sorry for him. He is leaving *his* house, *his* way of life, *his* children, *his* books. I feel the first stirrings of the guilty suspicion that *I* have failed *him*. That I am being unfair. I do not foresee, in my momentary empathy with Hank, how quickly he will locate a new apartment overlooking the park, buy a king-size bed, and find a woman to share it.

For my part, I am to learn that separation is no single point in time, but continues to happen over a long period—not only in the events themselves, which are often hurtful, but in the component parts of what was once a whole person, a whole life. I become a woman displaced socially and sexually; a single parent, no longer part of a team; a house-*wife*, whose "job" goes relentlessly on, but often mocks me.

My many parts, no longer unified by marriage, become charged with an energy released in the breakup; an energy expressed chiefly in anxiety, conflict, and depression. Separation becomes the central fact of my life.

Part One

Together

CHAPTER I

Portrait of a Marriage

The whole story is the meaning—because it is an experience, not an abstraction.

—FLANNERY O'CONNOR

HANK AND I spent exactly twenty years together—the core years of our lives; the years we waited for throughout childhood and youth; the years we would look back to in eventual stocktaking.

Our story, Hank's and mine, has the stabbing unity of any good drama: the themes and conflicts are there at the outset. The end is in the beginning—and throughout—in the ties and in the tears.

When we meet, Hank is twenty-nine and marriage-shy. I am twenty-five, and have turned down a series of men I find unsuitable. I seem most attracted to, most interested in men not interested in marrying me. I do not analyze why I want to marry Hank, but I do. He is boyish-looking, witty, considerate, ambitious. He is, I think, a husband for me. He is unhesitant about admiring me; about saying he finds me warm, vibrant, and attractive. We are comfortable with each other, congenial, laugh a lot. I think we will be good together, but Hank needs a year to come to this, to think it is *his* idea that we get married.

Once Hank capitulates, he is admiring, protective, loyal. It is I who become uncertain of my deeper feelings. In the last days before the wedding, I go through a grueling period of doubt, a wild desire to pull out. But I have no one to confess to; I simply let myself be carried forward by the plans and the prewedding celebrations. I do not resolve my doubts. I step over them—on my way to the altar.

The ceremony transforms Hank into an instant husband and I am graduated from a good girl to a good wife. It is incumbent upon me, I think, to make the marriage work; from the start, without putting it into words, I believe a failure would not only be intolerable, it would be *my* failure. Actually, we are anxious to please each other; to be mutual. The injunction of *our* day is "togetherness," not the "do your own thing" of today. We are an energetic, educated couple with humor and ambitions, entering the mainstream together. We are eager to be a "family," to explore our own abilities, interests, and the bewildering possibilities offered by our affluent society. We want it all. We take it all as our due: the deep involvement with work, children, a house of our own—success, in the model of the fifties and sixties. We have our unsuccesses: anxieties about money, a miscarriage of my first pregnancy, periods when Hank and I do not mesh. None of these stop us for long on our upwardly mobile curve.

In the early years, I am in constant motion. I move like a tornado through each day with its household tasks, my conscience and concern with our young children, my part-time work as a professional researcher in government. I fit in my leisure activities—tennis, music, time for friends—with enthusiasm, vigor, and a shoehorn! Hank is absorbed by the risk and challenge of starting his own business; he is also learning how to be a father to two baby girls, finding the way to relax and "enrich" his life. The days are long, and the years are short.

We have the usual Jack Sprat differences between a husband and wife. I am in motion because I like movement. Hank likes to sit—reading usually. Hank *watches* sports; I play tennis and take long walks. I like a cold bedroom; he wants a warm one. I am deliberate, analytic; Hank is quick and intuitive. He has the facts. I am in love with ideas. I'm big on ethics, and Hank shrugs off the moral issues—to decide matters more practically. I appear to do everything the hard way; I set impossibly high standards, which I then compel myself to meet. Hank, who is an only child, adheres to the pleasure principle; he simply turns away from what he does not wish to do.

We rock the boat from the first with our demands upon each other, our expectations, our sharply individualistic personalities. I am the perfectionist; Hank is the ritualist. I try hard to live up to his image of a wife who brings his slippers, talks gently and uncritically, smiling sweetly all the while. For weeks at a time I try earnestly to be Mrs. Miniver—but I'm not Greer Garson. With Hollywood's help, she does it so much better! All too often, I come a cropper of a lack of sweetness and light within me. And then I find: Hank is no Walter Pidgeon!

More important, neither of us has knowledge in our pores that marriage *can* be serene and affectionate. In each of the households from which we have come, we have been programmed for dissension and conflict. Yet with the eternal hubris of children toward their parents, we are convinced that *we* can do better, simply for the trying. We do not yet know that the imprint of our original homes, of the marriages in those homes, can be visited unto the second and the third generation.

Nothing is more token of our determination, of our times, than our turning to psychiatry for help. The role of psychiatry as an arbiter in the marriage is a chapter in itself. A significant chapter.

To document my memories, I turn the pages of the huge photograph album Hank and I once spent weeks assembling. To start off, there are yellowed clippings from *The New York Times* announcing our engagement, then our wedding, with the usual computerized facts, and no information. Then the wedding pictures, and pictures of our honeymoon, which show Hank on skis and skates for the first time. (He has not been to a snow resort since.) In the beginning pages, I am visibly buoyant and cheerful. I am tall, slender, with a great mass of auburn hair, a charge of expectancy and intensity that stirs the slick gravure paper. Hank is boyish, almost cherubic-looking. There is still very little time on his face; but his arms, even then, are protectively folded across his chest, his smiles are half questions—foretelling his later characterization of himself as "a brooding, introspective Jew—a loner."

Those pictures of the beginning years stir others, not in the album: the memory of sweet contentment and pleasure after we have been to bed with each other; of the quick, free laughter that makes the neighbors on the other side of the garden-apartment wall ask "What's always so funny at your place?"

When the babies come, we have the photographic clichés that become a sentimental treasure to us: I am bending over the bassinet bathing round, bald-headed infants; Hank and

I, in our Bermuda shorts, each hold a baby girl against our bare knees in an updated family tintype. I move in retrospect through Erika's and Jill's growing years: out of the back-yard wading pool onto the swings and jungle gym in the playground. We have pictures of the girls visiting the department-store Santa Claus for several years in a row: a clear progression from babies into little girls, from wonder to skepticism. We have snapshots of the girls taken with baby animals at the zoo, with summertime friends at camp, with historical monuments in New England, Williamsburg, and Washington. I am reminded, as I leaf through the album, that for years life with the children is omnipresent. They are my big job. I worry about Erika and Jill. I laugh with them, and cry over them.

Marriage is the fixed point while the children are growing. Yet amid the fullness of my days—the sound and fury of the girls' needs, the ringing of the telephone, the dozen times a day I turn the ignition key in the car—if I come to a stop, to a moment of silence, I am aware that the marriage is not quite "real," does not reach down to my roots. But I hold the door closed against too many daydreams, concentrate on my role as mother, housekeeper, and the helpful wife, lest I become restless and openly dissatisfied.

Hank wonders aloud about "life" in general, rather than about *our* life together. But we both unquestioningly assume that the tomorrow we are working toward, waiting for, will be more satisfying with each other, more serene. We have the viewpoint of the young, not ready to acknowledge the cynical wisdom of Yeats, that "all life is a preparation for something that never comes."

I turn more pages. My face and Hank's are no longer quite as smooth; our shapes are changing. But the photographs do not show waste. They show a family clowning, folk dancing at the school fair, celebrating anniversaries, birthdays, religious holidays—the passage of time.

In the last of the pictures, Erika and Jill are in their prom dresses and in their graduation robes. They stand in the curve of the path, in front of the maple we planted when they were babies—and the maple is now a full-limbed leafy tree. As I turn the pages, I see growth and change, as well as constancy in the fabric of our four lives. We are carried along by a momentum we have created. We have little need to take stock; we do not foresee the bankruptcy of a family.

But memories in the covert album of the mind are not all equally ritual and sentimental. Here are the dark twists and turns of doubts and unfulfilled yearnings. Here is the true ambivalence of the marriage, the San Andreas fault threatening to rip open the ground we tread together, day in and day out.

Hank's portrait of me is glowing and unflawed. But I know his view of me is a lie, and that one day I must surely be discovered in that lie. I see my humor, energy, boisterous affections as a huge put-on; beneath it all, the ineradicable underpainting of a hurt, defenseless child wanting from self-absorbed, quarrelsome, demanding parents the open affection, the acceptance that Hank is now offering. I need it, as I have always needed it; but even as I accept it from Hank, I feel chronically malcontent. Something in me is not satisfied; perhaps I have had the habit of unhappiness too long!

I dare not reveal myself. I contain my emotions tightly within my body walls, and behave more reasonably, more thoughtfully than ever. But I am a blatant romanticist; I like blue flowers on white china, the Schumann piano concerto, and tear-jerking movies. I do not recognize the contradiction in myself, the obvious displacement of emotions and desire.

Hank wants for himself the same total and uncritical acceptance he offers me. But this is not within me. I tell myself, reasonably, that I am accepting what is likable in Hank, rejecting what is not. Outwardly, I become more thoughtful than ever. I do more for him. But that is not what Hank is asking for. Yet I cannot give him what I cannot give myself: acceptance!

Hank has his own crosscurrents and contradictions, which I know full well. At work, he is funny, unruffled, handling the crises indigenous to his business skillfully, confidently, with a seeming ease and a clever quip. I love to visit him in his office; it is, I tell him, his natural habitat. There is some carry-over at home: he can be his own kind of Solomon, good-humored and detached when I am at my most intense, my most straight-faced, or untangling me when I am too caught up in Erika's and Jill's every problem. Except when he has his moods! Then Hank withdraws like a fire gone out. I reach over to share an event, a problem, an irony—and he isn't there. It begins as a lethargy, a nonresponsiveness, and builds until it becomes a strange, morose streak: the corrosive, evil genie he carries within him.

Hank's moods have a rhythm in their arrival and departure that can be felt throughout the house, usually twinned with unfounded concern for his physical well-being, with intense fear of financial insecurity. As time goes on, I tighten up at the first sign: the lethargy. I know that next Hank will turn a peeved, annoyed face toward me for something small, although ordinarily he has a delightful way of giving small things a very small place. Hank begins by being unhappy with himself; he ends by being unhappy with me. Inevitably, the mood builds into a large, explosive anger toward me.

I interact with Hank's moods as closely as the sandpiper follows the moving edge of the water. I am irritated, impatient, weighed down—and ashamed to acknowledge what I take to be a flaw in the man I married. If I stand back, I can see him as a lost child. But a lost child of thirty, then forty—almost fifty—has his bravado. Hank does not want to reveal or confess, except in rare, unguarded moments. So we do not talk much about it. He escapes into long hours of sleep and oblivion, but even there he is restless.

From the start, I hide my upset and "handle" Hank, as though he were an irascible, petulant child, another of my children. I dog my way through until the mood passes.

Once, without my customary caution, without stopping to consider my words with six-sided care, I protest: "Hank, I cannot be your psychiatrist!" He is so indignant, so hurt, that I retreat instantly; go back to crying secretly and trying harder. With both courage and cowardice, I hammer out a pattern of conciliation, avoidance, and coaxing that becomes my wife style.

In time I learn that the "moods" are depressions; serious depressions about which Dr. Aaron T. Beck, author of the definitive textbook on the subject, says:

> A depression in the marriage is deadly—a pervasive atmosphere of gloom, as impenetrable as a glass wall. What makes the situation so drastic is that you, the mate, cannot modify it, cannot reach through it. Whatever you do, whatever you say, he will eventually take the wrong way. Yet if you do nothing, you see him unravel before you. . . . A depression is quicksand: the harder you try, the farther down you go. Yet if you do nothing, you must sink anyhow!

For all my education, I lack the simple knowing I hear in a current country song: "When someone is unhappy with himself, he needs your love."

Love! Hank can and does say to me many, many times:

"I love you." But I cannot make the words come easily from my lips because my guilty secret, my deep-seated fear, is that what I feel for Hank is not love.

That is why, on the night of his forty-ninth birthday, when he cries out "nobody has ever loved me," I cannot give Hank the answer he wants. I want to love him, but love is my hang-up. I worry about the confusion, the inadequacy of my feelings. I worry that I am not capable of loving. I handle the word itself gingerly, as though it were out of the vocabulary of my experience. I know desire well enough, know what it is to be "crazy" about a man—always a man I cannot have. But this seems closer to infatuation, to Thomas Mann's definition of love as "a disease." I look upon love as something that other people feel, that I *should* feel. I want to conform, but love is a society in which I am not accepted, not initiated. It does no good to ask: Does Hank deserve my love? I know, even as an outsider, that love is its own excuse, its own act.

We are a going pair—albeit, perhaps, an odd couple—for most of the twenty years. We are not "marriers" who slide with seeming ease from one marriage into another. We consider one marriage real, two or more decreasingly so. We assume, despite the climate of divorce and the discouragement of marriage statistics, that *we* will have only this one marriage, that like the Momma and the Poppa ducks observed by naturalist Konrad Lorenz, we will squabble and squawk along, paired off for a lifetime. Hank is fond of quoting a line from *The Great Sebastians*, an old Lunt and Fontanne play: "I've thought of murder, but never divorce!"

What holds us together? The conventions of marriage? Inertia? Hank's acceptance of whatever belongs to him? His chivalry, his gallantry, his home-centered make-up? And what holds me? Lack of courage to leave? Fear of financial insecurity? More, I want to believe. For when I have recited

2 5

the moods, the doubts, the flaws, I am still giving only one part. There is another.

There is simply too much in the marriage for me to leave. We spend the years moving together; ironically, we even move past each other, so that I become a bit more easygoing, even slightly lazy, while Hank becomes compulsive, almost organized. As I begin to worry, to be anxious, he becomes less so. We pick up bits of each other's speech, adopt each other's expressions and gestures. At the start, I am the liberal in raising the children; by the time we part, he is outliberaling, outphilosophizing me.

Until our last months, he would reach for my hand in the darkened theater and remind me during the frightening, brutal scenes: "It's only a movie." He teaches me about the masculine world of earning a living, tells me dirty jokes, and breaks down some of the priggish manners that come with my "dignity." Tenderly and patiently, he teaches me everything I know about sex. He offers me the shelter and sweetness I did not find in my childhood home.

When things are going well between us—"prosperity," Hank calls it—I am happy with my lot. Certainly happier than I have been other places, other times. In this state of grace, I give out bounteously, easily—and Hank gets the lion's share.

I turn to him, at these times, in gratitude, warmed to the very center of my being, radiating warmth back toward him in a pleasure and contentment I express through cooking, tending, giving gifts—my characteristic way of giving myself. I am tied by his generosity toward me; by his calm, which contrasts with the peaks of my enthusiasm, the high horses of anger in my more flamboyant make-up.

But a time comes when the coin is turned over. Hank's introspection and self-searching turn to dissatisfaction and unbridled restlessness, and as always, I become its focus, its target. What Hank once saw as my vitality, my strong life-force, now becomes, to him, an unbearable aggressiveness. "You are too much for me, I cannot take it," he says. I dare not reply that he is "not enough" for me, but I, too, am defiant.

CHAPTER II

Scenes in a Marriage

> . . . and will you have the desire to behold and
> to comprehend those things for which there is
> no need to travel, in the presence of which you
> stand here and now, each one of you? Will you
> not realize then who you are and to what end
> you are born and what this is you have received
> the power to see?
>
> —EPICTETUS

AFTER THE breakup, the psychiatrist asks: "When did
your marriage die, Eve?" I recoil from the words, which are
too final for me. But my mind scurries about, searching hur-
riedly. Which time does he mean? He tells me: "When you
went to Italy."

But it is, in truth, not Italy alone, but Italy and Paris; it is
hotel rooms in many cities, our own bedroom, a room in
the hospital whose walls I studied for several months. Each
place is part of the death, if, indeed, it is a true death.

Italy is an episode in our lives I have been meaning to
understand, a negative I mean to develop.

Italy. Hank and I are part of the rash of American families that take a year abroad in the sixties. We want a sabbatical from our daily lives. We arrive in Rome ahead of schedule, without reservations, without living accommodations. It is a Sunday in October. It is siesta time, and the temperature is 93 degrees. The city is as shuttered and somnolent as any provincial town. But the quiet is deceiving. The tourist season is *not* over. The only accommodation we can find is an expensive hotel of Marienbad vintage, all dusty plush and an air of genteel, overaged poverty. Not recommended for suburban American children used to slamming in and out of the kitchen door.

With the hotel as an uncomfortable base, we search diligently, fruitlessly for an apartment. Rome is crowded with American families evacuated from the Middle East in another crisis. Just when we think we have seen, and rejected, our last seedy apartment, we find a freshly painted, underfurnished flat facing the Tiber. The afternoon we move in, young neighborhood boys in short pants follow Erika with approving murmurs of *"bella, bella."*

I am absorbed with settling in, with shopping, with coping in my Berlitz Italian. But I am not too busy to notice that Hank is growing uneasy, restless. The novelty of Rome is palling. Now that he has shepherded us from the United States, found us an apartment, his work is done. He spends more and more time in the *studio* leafing through books and magazines that he does not read.

I write home to Julia Borden, my closest friend:

> I think Rome is going to fizzle. The truth is I think
> Hank is sorry he started the whole thing, and is ready to
> call it quits. Each morning I wake up determined to carry

him along with my good cheer, but he is so morose that in an hour I could cut my throat. As for Erika and Jill—they are happy and busy at school from eight in the morning until four-thirty in the afternoon. On weekends, they have neighborhood friends who are learning to speak English and drink Coca-Cola in our apartment.

Hank announces that he wants to go home. My resentment is instant and fierce. I am stubbornly determined to have this time in Italy now that we are here. I suggest, reasonably, as always: "You go home, and I'll stay on with the girls until the first semester ends in January . . ." My words fade off. I can see that Hank is hurt and angry. He wants me to be his Ruth, to go unhesitatingly where he goes. I try more words, try justifying myself. He is cold, cold, cold, and I can no longer contain my anger, conceal my resentment. I blurt out: "This does not bode well for our future." I sound threatening, but it is no more than the sound of an empty tin can rattling down the street!

Hank does go home alone, but before he leaves, he must procure a new, separate passport. We have been traveling together on a family passport, our four faces crowded into the small regulation-sized square. The clerk at the American Embassy now takes our passport from Hank, studies it, writes out many forms in triplicate, and, as a finale, he marks a great X over the face of our family picture and stamps two new, separate passports. The moment is heavy and sick with symbolism. A small divorce.

On our last night together in the great Italian *letto di marito*, each of us lies stiffly in his own half of the bed. We do not touch so much as a toe of each other's.

I see Hank off on the Rome-Paris Express, and instead of relief I find I am fighting off my awareness of his anger. I am no longer so defiant, no longer so *sure* I have the right to remain behind. I begin an empty, lonely time. I do not think out the possibility that this will be a break. I do not dare. I expend most of my energy fighting back my anxiety.

Hank stays with the Bordens his first weeks at home. Actually, while Julia is my closest friend, John and Julia are *our* best friends. John and Hank became friends when they worked on their college newspaper together. Julia and I were "new girls in town" who met each other at work. The inexorable operation of the boy-girl network brought us all together on a first double date, and thus began an unusual four-way friendship. Collectively, in the next years, we live through some prosperity and some recession, through six successful births, one miscarriage and one abortion, as well as the threat of cancer, endocarditis, and ulcerative colitis. The years bring us an intimacy and relaxation, family-style privileges and family manners. The Bordens' marriage goes in tandem with ours—a sibling marriage.

My one-to-one friendship with Julia is beyond Worcestershire sauce and such; we are concerned with the psyches of our children, our marriages, our interrupted "careers." Long before women's liberation, we are concerned with the core dilemma of being married and yet being one's self. We are an oddly contradictory pair of friends. I look far more extroverted and talkative, while Julia's the quiet one. Yet it is I who am reticent, and Julia who is totally open. When she begins to complain about John, about the trap that marriage has become for her, she mistakenly takes my discreet silence for an equal discontent. This explains, in part, the role Julia plays in the Italian episode—and later, in the separation.

When Hank returns home from Italy, he makes Julia his confidante, and she writes to me:

Hank has told me all, and I mean all—and frankly, I don't have any answers for you.

Hank is angry, disgusted, bitter, and deeply hurt. He saw as much of Italy as he wanted to see, in fact, as much as he could stand. He is very happy to be home, and working, and seeing his friends. People are happy to see *him*. To report, factually, the general social reaction: He was right to come home, and the decision shows matureness.

Hank now has a studio apartment. He is not pining away for you as far as I can see. He already has about him the attractive, gay look of the untied bachelor. And he gets a lot of heat and light and hot water and good American steaks—and he isn't going to be cold at night. Anger is not the same as sadness and loneliness. You can keep real warm on anger.

I can only tell you what the realities seem at this end. It is up to you to compare them with your own realities.

John wants me to ask you the only important question: Do you *want* Hank?

Not until eight years afterward, walking on a beach only sixty miles from my home, will I finally ask—with the deepest penetration possible—What *do* I want? and learn that the answer is Hank.

During the Christmas holidays, I drive the girls to Naples, Pompeii, Sorrento. When we return to Rome, a cable is waiting under the door: "Come home immediately. Enough of this. Hank." With idiotic haste, I make arrangements to pack and fly home. I dare not, as I sit between Erika and Jill on the long flight home, think what it will be like to face Hank again. I am unsure of what to say or to do. I am numb. At the New York airport, we sort each other out after the customs and immigration lines. Hank kisses me. But he remains cool and guarded. He is ebullient with the children.

It is 3 A.M. Too late for the long car ride home. We check into a New York hotel. In bed, Hank wants me. There are no questions, no healing words, and I feel his hurt and anger through the reunion of sex. I am his wife and he needs me. But I am also the naughty little girl who did not mean to be naughty, who is confused because the adults call her naughty!

The next morning we drive home. With each day that passes, the familiar closes over the months in Italy like an incoming tide taking down a sand castle. Although Hank asks me more than once: "Can you explain it to me?" I feel that he is not asking, but accusing. I do not want to defend myself for fear that I will attack. We never talk it out, but Hank's anger and hurt dissipate gradually in the seeming "normality."

Italy never comes to rest between us. It remains an incomplete gestalt, its tensions and ramifications all too ready to spring to life again. I find myself reaching frantically for new work, new study courses, new recreations. Each new interest pulls me a little farther from Hank, a little farther along my own way. It is no accident that travel becomes an issue between us. Whenever we are not doing well together, I have the need to "travel," to see other places, mingle with other lives. And I go without Hank.

I do not agree with the psychiatrist. The marriage does not *die* in Italy. But something romantic, something hopeful is lost: the unfocused vision of happiness toward which we were striving, together. Italy means facing the differences in our make-up; differences that anger us, wrench us apart. Italy is a mere forecast, a separation in miniature, just as the scene in the New York hotel room is one of many such scenes we play out in the next years: Hank taking what he needs and wants from me, demanding more and more; and I, all the while, trying desperately to determine what Hank means to me, what he offers me, what he takes away—and where he leaves me as a woman.

Paris. That is where I believe the heart of the marriage stops. For me, Paris is the point of no return. On a Saturday morning, in a hotel on the Left Bank. I may remember the cabbage roses on the wall of that room as long as I live.

I am on another trip, stopping in Paris on my way home from Israel and Greece. This time, as a pretext for traveling, I take Erika and Jill. Hank joins us in Paris for the last five days. I am glad to see him. It is good to share a room, a bed, a meal with him after several weeks alone with the girls, who are full of their teen-age interests and selves. Hank is not restless; we are enjoying ourselves in the museums, the good restaurants, the shops. On the morning I am talking of, the Saturday, Hank is feeling sleepily amorous. But it is my last day. I want to dress and go out. But he is insistent; he will not be turned away. I do not have the bodily ease for sex, yet I do not want to turn him down; that always leaves an unhappy miasma between us. I give in; soon, I become involved and put away my nagging wish to be elsewhere. I follow and respond to his desire.

Suddenly, Hank says: "You'll never change!" His words carry an inutterable dissatisfaction, a discontent, a rejection of what I *can* offer him.

The moment stands, a lodestone in my mind and heart. In that old-fashioned French bed, with the morning light gentle and soft, the curtains stirring voluptuously, I give up hope. In that moment, I give up the struggle to make it better between us.

By the time I get onto the plane that evening, I am sick with unhappiness. I am beginning to have symptoms of the threatening sickness about which I had already been warned.

At home, the illness speeds up at a crazy, unpredicted rate, and I am soon in the hospital, on the critical list, where I remain for a long while. No one, nothing, seems able to *make* me well. Under the impact of the drugs and the illness, I am not always sane. But I hear with absolute clarity when Hank sits by my bed and tells me: "Get better! Just get better. I will let you go, if you wish."

I did not know he knew: that I was unhappy, restless, captive.

The illness drags on drearily, but when I finally do get well, neither of us again mentions Hank's "offer." I put it off because I think I cannot afford to open this Pandora's box. But, in the end, Hank opens it, in his own way.

I persuade myself, in what is to be our last months together, that it is "just" another bad time, angry, hurtful, and joyless; that the pendulum will swing back, inexplicably, to one of our better times. The pattern will repeat itself. Hasn't it always?

This time the reality changes. Day by day we lose ground. My throat tightens. My shoulders ache. I clench my hands in the dark of the movies, and I cannot let go of my smile, although my face is stiff and tired. I have the classic look, for anyone who wishes to see, of one more woman on the outskirts of marital defeat.

Hank is no happier. He is *un*smiling, his face heavy with anger and self-defeating introspection. "Change! Change, you will have to change!" he commands me. I cannot grasp what he wants of me. I am disoriented by his vague accusations, jolted out of focus by the ultimatum. I am no longer at ease, even with myself.

At the dinner table, in those last weeks, our voices and our postures are barricaded against each other. The food, for me, is laden with Hank's discontent and displeasure. I cower against the wall of my own thoughts. I handle Hank's sullen, angry silence as I might an ugly wound; covering it discreetly with "safe" islands of conversation. I am grateful for Erika and Jill, for their attempts to outtalk each other at the table. The girls do not apparently sense what is wrong. But one evening Erika catches me off guard: "You look so sad, Mommy!"

I take long walks, as though the physical act could, in itself, outdistance the unhappiness; but it is always there, waiting, when I return. I go to New York for a day to break the ugly momentum. But I cry in the Palm Court of the Plaza. I join a tour to Europe, and cry in a small café along the Seine. Whether I return in a day or a month, the discontent is still laced into the atmosphere, locked into our lives.

I tell myself I do not *have to* stay. I do not *have to* continue to suffer. I do not *have to* remain married to a man who rejects all joy, all possibility of joy, in an endless, brooding depression. I want to cop out. To escape.

In my mind, I have many times—without ever making a move. I do not know how I can leave my marriage anymore than I know how I can leave my skin.

When Hank tells me *he* is thinking of leaving, I discover that I do not know how to "separate." I am a professional researcher, working for both industry and government in the field of population. But all of my training, all the common sense and practicality of my make-up are mired in unhappiness. I am too proud, at this point, to confide in friends; too private to walk into a mahogany office hung with Daumier prints and tell a strange lawyer the intimate details of our lives, a story of failure he has undoubtedly heard only too often before.

Nothing gives a better indication of my state of mind, of my naïveté at this point, than my first effort to seek advice.

I go to the local office of the Legal Aid Society, thinking I can remain private and seek information at the same time.

"Whaddyawant?" the receptionist in the Legal Aid office asks, not bothering to look up from her typewriter. I pay my two-dollar registration fee, which enables me to consult a staff lawyer, and receive number Eighteen. Two hours and twenty minutes later I am still waiting to see a lawyer, still sitting in a stiff-backed chair in a line of stiff-backed chairs occupied by men in their shirt sleeves, and one woman. She is wearing curlers and ankle socks. I leave.

The next week I make an appointment with one of the few lawyers among our friends. He is Matthew Post, a soft-spoken, genial man who is the lawyer for Hank's firm. Still guarding my privacy, ashamed to admit that Hank is threatening to leave me, aware that Hank would be furious if he knew I'd come, I tell Matthew "the marriage is deteriorating," and ask what I should do.

"What do you mean 'deteriorating'? Use plain terms."

I tighten up at Matthew's unexpected brusqueness, at the implied rebuke. The word "deteriorating," which makes no sense to Matthew, signifies with exactness the pall over our house and our lives.

No "plain terms" are more germane to me than the fierce reality of my strained emotions. But ahead of me are the worldly lessons in objectivity and the law, in economics and the underside of human nature—including my own. Matthew gives me the first factual, objective lesson. As *our* friend, he can be lawyer to neither of us. However, if we *agree* to separate and come to him together, he can then write a "friendly" separation agreement. With glorious irrelevance, he tells me that if we are divorced, I can use my "own" name again.

I only half hear what Matthew is telling me. I am superstitious, convinced that by putting my fears into words, I have now made separation possible.

I am irrational, but right. There is no going back. No swing of the pendulum. Within two weeks after my visit to Matthew Post, Hank walks out.

Part Two
Alone

CHAPTER III

Getting Unmarried

It is impermissible, nay fatal, to be personal and
undesirable.

—MARIANNE MOORE

I DO NOT see Hank. I do not talk to him. There is only
silence between us now. I am floating free—released from
his anger, from pressures. After twenty years in which I per-
suaded, arranged, and apologized to get my way, I experience the novelty of saying what I think, of going where I
wish, seeing whom I please. I am conscious of a new sensation: I own myself!

But what once seemed so desirable soon loses the sharp,
intoxicating edge of pleasure, and I begin to ask: What am I
free *for*?

I become disoriented. Numb. My senses do not respond.
The early-morning light, the first hot, dark taste of coffee, the
cardinal flashing its red against the green of the holly—the
simple pleasures of my senses—cannot stir me, cannot pene-
trate the numbness. I turn away from poetry and from fic-
tion, seemingly unable to tolerate intensity and emotion. I
think my capacity to be moved, to be aroused, has been de-

stroyed. Alone at bedtime, I am tired, eager for long, long hours of sleep. I have no need for tears, and I wonder: "Shouldn't I be feeling this more?"

I need not have worried! Once I can no longer outrun myself, the numbness thaws into a rage of feeling. My mind begins a *"mea culpa"* that swells to a blaring, dissonant rag. I do not have the tough-hided, self-preserving impulse to tell myself it was Hank's fault—and believe it for more than five consecutive minutes! I wear an invisible scarlet letter *S* for separation, the mark of the woman who could not hold her marriage together.

Now that it is gone, I become obsessed with the need to judge the marriage. I see it now through my eyes, now through Hank's, now through the chance but revealing words of a friend. If I tell myself we were not a Romeo and Juliet, but a marriage, like any other, with built-in weaknesses and strengths, I can find no consolation in its ending; only a sense of loss. If I see it as a bad marriage, which should have been dissolved sooner, then I am left with the intolerable picture of wasting "the best years of our lives," of raising two children in the maleficent aura of failure. I am playing a game of grim sorts, without a possibility of winning. But this search for some fixed truth, for some assignment of blame, is an almost universal after-torment of a broken marriage.

Sometimes I become audience to myself: as I talk, as I act, I find myself seeing and hearing with *Hank's* eyes, with *Hank's* ears. I continue to shadowbox against his disapproval. The twenty years hang stubbornly on and I have no defense against the part of him he last left behind, within me.

The nighttime becomes continuous with the mood of the day, frenetic, jagged, no longer an escape. Asleep, I search for something lost; I miss trains; and I dream I am not, never have been, married. In the morning I resurface and breathe in sharply, to find the confusions, the fears of the day waiting on my pillow. I face myself as a woman stranded and alone.

"You're feeling sorry for yourself," the psychiatrist tells me. I know. And yet, I am not without the exquisite, saving contradiction of a woman. Throughout my high-pitched woes, I wonder, with a tinge of excitement: "Can I start over with another man? Am I still desirable? Will I find someone? Will I marry a second time?" I do not stop to think that I am not yet out of the first marriage!

I return home after a weekend in New York to find that in my absence Hank has come by. He has taken a bridge table, the better of our portable typewriters, his humidor, and an abstract painting we bought on our first vacation together. His presence in the house, his having been there, jars me. He should have asked. He had no right! I become self-righteous. Indignant. For a moment I consider changing the lock on the front door. Then I think: "No, why shouldn't he have the few things? He's taken very little thus far." I am still reasonable enough, guarded enough, to say nothing, do nothing. That same quality that makes me stiff-necked with pride also make me determined not to bicker, not to make a tasteless to-do over small matters.

"Do you want him back?" my friend Marya asks as we drive down to the seashore for the day. I am astonished by the bluntness of her question but fend her off with the careful and protective reply, "I'm not sure yet."

Odd as it may seem, I have not asked *myself* Marya's direct question. I am still learning what separation is, still catechizing myself on my failure, and living with the simple, dumb wish that "this" could be over. I am living through the classic sequence of relief, guilt, and regret.

But what *do* I want? My answer is an unbidden, recurring daydream: Hank needs me again; he will come back. Once more he will put a protective arm about me and shield me from the frightening world into which I have been catapulted. In the comfort of the daydream, I am no longer frightened.

Imperceptibly, my thinking shifts to ". . . if he comes back." Gradually, the meaning is forced upon me. No matter what I say to others, or even to myself, *I believe Hank will be back*. I do not yet know that *every* woman believes the husband who walks out will be back. I have little use for every woman, no room for her in the egocentricity of my upset. Nor do I take account of Hank's new existence until I must, eventually, face the facts.

"Can I talk with one of the kids?" I pick up the telephone on a sleepy Saturday afternoon and am startled into wakefulness. It is Hank. This is the first time since he left that I hear his voice. My heart pounds. My throat closes, so that I reply in a small, forced voice, "No, they're both out."

"Please ask Jill or Erika to call me." I am not quick enough to say something, anything. He hangs up, and it's over. Did I miss an opportunity? The chasm grows larger. The quality of the silence is bleak. I cannot tolerate the emptiness. That week I go blocks out of my way to pass Hank's office building, hoping he will appear on the street, yet dreading a chance encounter. As I stand there—ten seconds, ten minutes; I do not know—he does not appear. I tell myself I am childish, neurotic, hysterical. But these are mere words and cannot contain me. I want to see Hank. I am trapped in the myth of what might have been, what should have been, more remote each day from the angers and attri-

44

tion of reality. I do not yet ask, as I can later, whether it is the shelter of marriage I miss and want or Hank himself.

With consummate timing, the census taker arrives in this period. I answer her questions, and she moves our "family" into the broken-homes column. The experience is but one of the small, touchy tasks of getting unmarried. I must break the news to my mother, keep my manner toward Hank's dad "friendly" and unreproachful, tell friends, one by one, before they hear about us in a casual telling at the next dinner party. I must fight off caring what people will say, reminding myself that we will certainly not be news for long, that our happening will soon be supplanted with fresher, more titillating material.

The girl scout in me helps, keeping me busy and useful. I lean hard on habit, on the semiautomatic moving parts that cook, clean, and launder. I exploit my vanity, my narcissism, my desire to live. With a woman's shrewdness, I recognize that desperation will feed on my spirit and vitality—and will show in my face! I fight against paralysis and self-pity with so many long walks that my poodle slinks under a chair when I reach for his leash. I play tennis and, ironically, my game has never been better. At times, I am caught up, almost happy, in familiar activities. It is not all grim.

A friend sends me a new book on separation and divorce, literally a how-to handbook. As in all advice books, the problems are not precisely mine, the solutions too general to apply. But two of the author's suggestions stay with me. (1) Cream your face religiously, and (2) refrain from saying nasty things about your erstwhile husband.

I begin at once to cream my face compulsively. But I know, even before reading the handbook, that I would be unwise

45

to accuse Hank, to justify myself, to discuss my private affairs publicly. I have my own prototypes of how *not* to behave. One is a woman I met on my European trip who told me that her husband often struck her, that he was attempting to "gaslight" her, that he was having an unhidden affair. Even as I write, that wife is still living with that same husband, still "leaving." The other how-not-to is a composite; she is the woman I meet in the supermarket or the beauty parlor who thinks that because *her* husband walked out, too, that we are instant sorority sisters. She tells me variously that her husband is a pathological liar, that he is neglecting the children, that he is bilking the common-property fund. I listen, curious, even greedy, for confirmation that I am not alone.

But everything urges *me* to be quiet: wisdom, taste, and the fact that I am not in a position to talk. I am the discarded wife, suspect for my shortcomings. Perhaps I am also protecting what little is left, keeping it possible to move backward if . . .

I have a rationalization for my behavior. I call it *la bella figura*, and I learned it from a twenty-year-old girl who did housework for me in Italy. At seven in the morning, this young woman would put on her lipstick and eye make-up, straighten her stocking seams, cinch the belt of her trench coat, simply to go to the corner café for milk and fresh rolls. I asked her once why she took such pains. It was, she explained, *la bella figura*—putting the best possible face on things. I did not learn the philosophy in Italy, but simply a name for it!

I may only *think* I am putting up a front. Friends tell me I am "remarkable," but it remains for Erika's current young man to tell me, months later: "Now you sound like yourself. This summer you were not real!"

Yet, for others, my pose works too well. I walk into a room where two of my good friends are talking. They become uncomfortably silent and then confess: "We've been talking about *you*. We don't understand. You laugh, you joke. You don't show anything. How can you act as though nothing has happened?" At that moment, I hate them for being taken in. Ironically, I am put on the defensive because I'm *not* in tears. Yet I know full well they would not enjoy seeing me let go. The full force of my feelings would be too much, "too emotional"—a phrase all of us use handily for someone else's suffering. I prefer the forthrightness of another friend who does not call me for several months; when she does, finally, she confesses: "I was shying away from your pain!"

For all my determination and will, my style is by no means foolproof. I want desperately to handle myself with dignity, but there is little comfort in dignity. My guard and tongue slip, little by little. When I am asked "What happened?" I will sometimes say "Hank is having a bad attack of middle age." But after I say this a few times, I realize I am no less hostile than my own negative models. When I am asked even more direct questions: "Does Hank have somebody else? Do you?" "Do you think you'll get together again?" I must fight back the emotion that lies in wait like some guerrilla force. The problems—money, my future, the dread of a flat tire as I drive alone at night—all feed my self-pity, my irrational need to see Hank as the villain who walked out, and to see myself as the slightly tragic, abandoned figure. This is palliative nonsense, I know, as outmoded as the operetta, at odds with everything I think in "normal" times about marriage, about relations between men and women. Yet I need to hear friends tell me it's Hank's loss, that they're *my* friends more than *his*. I want

47

Erika and Jill on my side, although the notion of "sides" between parents violates every thought, every effort Hank and I have put into their upbringing. I will come back to the sensitive matter of the children at a later point.

One person refuses to take sides. She is Julia Borden, who continues to see Hank as she always has—a human being with his needs, eccentricities, and reasons. Exactly the judicious, well-balanced stand I might take if I were the onlooker rather than the participant! In the last months that Hank was at home, Julia had been in the habit of calling him in his office, telling him her problems with John. Hank responded, I would guess, by telling Julia his problems. They began to have an occasional dinner together. I thought then that it would help Hank to have someone to talk with. I did not realize that this could become a booby trap for me. Not in the obvious way. Not that Julia and Hank become lovers— to my knowledge. They simply become the unhappiness kids! Merely by listening, they support and justify each other—like ersatz psychiatrists.

In the period immediately after separation, Julia is my only link with Hank, the only person who talks with both of us. She mentions Hank casually, without realizing that her smallest reference magnifies, distorts, resounds in the emptiness I am experiencing. Julia expects me to accept her posture of fairness as effortlessly as she assumes it.

"Hank's marvelous these days," she tells me. "Freedom agrees with him. He's not angry anymore—just angry with you." And she informs me, "If you think he's coming back, you're wrong."

In a voice that is unnaturally quiet and controlled, I respond, "Julia, what makes you think I want to hear all this?"

In her open way, which can be as endearing as it is unwise and indiscreet, she accedes instantly. "You're right. I won't mention Hank again."

I do not make a dramatic break with Julia. I cannot simply discard the friendship, dump it peremptorily in the Goodwill collection box along with the rumpled ties and frayed shirts Hank leaves behind. Nevertheless, I allow myself a private, teeth-clenching anger toward Julia—all the anger I cannot permit myself toward Hank. I withdraw gradually from sharing confidences with Julia, from the easy interchange of more than twenty years, and in so doing, I close down the place where I have always been most forthright, most myself. It is a place I sorely miss.

Luckily, I have other friends who form a warm, supportive claque. I know that many women after separation feel naked and unprotected in the living rooms where they were once "couples." Others complain of neglect, because they are not invited, because they present the extra-woman problem to the hostess. But I am asked, and I go. In truth, I enjoy myself. I relish the attention, the role—no matter how I underplay it—of the slightly wronged woman.

But I become conscious of the new, small niceties of my position. It would be bad manners and bad friends to appear too conversational with, too absorbed in, someone else's husband—the same behavior that only a month or two before would not have warranted a second thought. When another woman's husband escorts me to the car, kisses me good night, locks the door and cautions me to drive carefully, it is sweet of him. But once per husband is enough.

When I start my car, the party is over. I am shunted back to aloneness. I am raw and self-conscious about going home without a man, going home to an empty bedroom.

Yet a small part of me knows I am dramatizing. I have

49

been married long enough, observed other marriages closely enough, to know that the moment back together in the car can literally signal the "end" of an evening, that the letdown often takes only a word, a lift of the eyebrow to set in motion discontent, dissatisfactions, even a quarrel. What *am* I mourning for?

CHAPTER IV

The Panic Button

WOMAN CLIENT: Do I have grounds for divorce?
WOMAN LAWYER: Grounds? You're married,
aren't you?

—REPORT OF A CONVERSATION

HANK ASKS me, the last time we sit together in the breakfast room: "How much money will you need?"

I make a tight fist of my feelings. With a cunning self-protectiveness that I experience for the first, but not for the last time, I know instantly I am not equipped to protect myself. To talk about money as Hank is leaving would be to go into battle without a second. I am at a disadvantage. I will not discuss money matters. Hank says: "I plan to take care of you, but I intend to do it voluntarily. I don't like to be pushed. You know I can get nasty if I'm pushed."

Yes. I know.

Hank begins to send me a weekly check that covers food and out-of-pocket expenses, something less than the house money I am accustomed to, but I manage. I fancy I am living "in the meantime," although I have no concept of what comes next. Hank pays the mortgage and the utility bills.

I can see now, as I could not then, how this might seem logical to him: I am not out on the street. Neither is he; he is living, temporarily, in one of the better apartment-hotels in town. I am still concerned with the "bigger" issues of separation, still in limbo, and money is the smallest part of the limbo. I even sense that Hank is trapped, forced to support me and a household he no longer wants.

Then comes a note in Hank's very small, very neat handwriting. No salutation. Simply the message: "I will not pay any bills contracted after June 12."

The bills are routine: for grass cutting, department-store purchases, household repairs, and the long et cetera of any going household. This is not the "I plan to take care of you" with which he left.

His note pushes the panic button. I think money, money, money. How will we live? Who will pay the bills? Money breaks me out into a cold sweat, into a near hysteria that will take months to calm, that will make me behave in ways I cannot honor in myself; it enters into my relationship with the children, fuels a vicious, though hidden vendetta against Hank, and even rekindles resentments toward my father, now dead, and toward my mother.

I assume I should see a lawyer. After my experience with Matthew Post, I do not want a friend! Through hearsay, I choose a man named Alan Springer. From the start, Alan is easy to talk with, not exasperatingly cautious with his words, not showing signs of being wearied by my oft-told tale or being antagonistic to women in the hidden ways reputedly characteristic of divorce lawyers. He's a decent human being, both in the practice of law and in his own life, and, as he reminds me, he's "been through it." He's been married before. Now in his young forties, he has the lean, wiry look of a tennis player, the lean, wiry mind of a man able to defend himself—and me! I have the sensation that at last somebody is on *my* side, and the relief brings embarrassing tears.

I am subdued, at first, by the well-bred environment of Alan's old-line, conservative office: old-fashioned leather chairs, maroon carpeting, and black no-nonsense lettering on the opaque glass doors. The inevitable Daumiers. I dress discreetly for my appointments with Alan, lean forward in my chair when Alan speaks. I am attentive, learning the lessons of my legal position; a new pupil, intent upon pleasing the teacher.

"It is my job to protect you. You are the innocent party," Alan tells me.

I protest that no one is innocent in a marriage, but I am playing devil's advocate. He is the "poor-me" fantasy in legal dress.

Yet I have the odd, alienated sensation that I am a job applicant, applying hard for a job I do not want. The law, from the start, is my private comedy of the absurd. The *E. Baguedor v. H. Baguedor* file set out on Alan's desk is far less "real" than my inner chaos. In months to come, as each incident fissions into other incidents, each phone call begets other phone calls, I watch the file fatten on conflict, grow thick—and expensive. And much later, when I begin to see Hank semifurtively, I find it impossible to tell Alan. I have the bizarre sensation that I am cheating on the file, being unfaithful to my lawyer.

Alan's consolations—that "others have lived through this," "everybody I've ever known is better off two years later"— acknowledge obliquely that he knows my heart is sinking, that I am having trouble living in a half-empty bedroom, eating at a manless dinner table. But Alan's task is neither confidences nor sympathy; it is, as he assures me, "protection."

Alan recommends that we work toward a separation agreement; he would counsel divorce if he could ensure my financial security. I turn cold with dread at the mention of divorce. I am neither clear nor logical. I do not have Hank, but I cannot accept the finality of divorce. From the beginning, I cannot let go.

I am both enlightened and threatened as I learn that I am vulnerable. My choice of action is almost nonexistent; my rights, slender. "The law in our state is not protective of women," Alan informs me; there is no provision for division of assets, for alimony, for sharing property. I must wait until Hank wants a divorce, until he wants to "trade" for it.

If Hank does not volunteer a fair income for the girls and for me by signing a *de facto* agreement—which would bind him to a set amount of money each month—I can go into court and charge nonsupport. The judge will then decide what is "enough"; his decision will be incorporated into a court order. Hank must pay the monthly sum designated or go to jail.

The focus, the talk, the negotiations have only one sight: money; this is the precise synonym for the "protection" Hank is to provide willy-nilly. As an addendum, Alan says that "the agreement will allow each of you to go your own way." In the meanwhile, he cautions, in an old-world manner, that my behavior must be discreet. In short; I am not to be seen with another man. This is so irrelevant, I hardly listen. Later, when it should concern me, I do not remember being warned. But by then, I am in no mood to be cautious.

Alan points out the possibility that I will never marry again. Men in my age group are looking for women ten, even twenty years younger. So much for my imaginings! I confidently assure Alan that Hank is *not* involved with another woman, but Alan is equally confident: "He soon will be. No man in his position stays alone for long." He gives me the comfort and capstone of his thinking: "Once a marriage reaches the lawyer's office, it's Humpty Dumpty, and cannot be put back together again."

I am dependent for my total financial existence on Hank's signing an agreement. But, by its nature, an agreement is never easy to reach, never satisfying to either side. For the wife, the payments are never "enough" to live on; for the husband, the monthly check must always seem "too much." Why should Hank sign an agreement? Conscience? Never a reliable motivation, conscience becomes less and less active as it is removed farther from its prod. A divorce? If Hank were to sign the agreement, and then decide he wants a divorce, he would have nothing left to "trade." Yet the law prohibits us from making one package: an agreement *with* preprovision for possible future divorce. Such an arrangement is considered conspiracy under the law.

I have only one trump: taking Hank into court. At the beginning I consider this nothing more than a useful threat, a rattling of sabers, never an actual possibility, never as something that will come to pass. But neither do I foresee on those first low-keyed visits to Alan Springer how important the legal aspects will become, that negotiations, telephone calls, minor incidents will build into a real-life drama and a shrill crescendo. I do not foresee how fully I will get into the swing of controversy.

"How does an intelligent woman like you leave herself in this position?" Alan asks as he reviews my personal assets. They are close to zero.

"Easily," I answer, to myself. It simply did not occur to me to protect myself *against* Hank. It was *he* who was sheltering me from economic hardship and insecurity. The job of living within our income amid all of our "necessities" was challenge enough. I did not squirrel away private amounts of money for myself; any money I earned I threw into the mutual pot for a new rug, a couch, a holiday. I could hardly be less sharing than Hank, who shared everything with us. Until he *became* the emergency, he met them all.

It is, ironically, not accumulated property or wealth we are talking about; it is only what Hank is capable of earning. I am still close enough to "our" financial picture to know there is not a lump sum of money put away for college, although Alan says "the agreement must provide for the girls' college educations and your medical bills." The money that might now be securely in the bank has already gone: for psychiatric bills, private-school bills, flute lessons, piano lessons, ballet lessons, and, the largest sums of all for Hank's illness of a few years back (he was in the hospital for a month; at home for two months more) and mine, which began soon after my return from Israel, and stretched out through a long, black year. The cost of our illnesses, we once calculated, could keep both Erika and Jill in college for two years. I also know that if my illness should flare again, Hank's health insurance would cover only part of the possible bills.

How will we manage? The "we" is unintentional. I am still thinking backward, not yet out of the habit of thinking of the money as a shared problem. Although we had our differences over money—I was the more extravagant; Hank, the more anxious about money—it was not a tense area. Hank was generous and did not question me closely on my expenditures. He had no appetite for pursuing or saving small sums. I would often find a rich lode of change and crumpled bills along with loose bits of pipe tobacco when I sent his suits to the cleaner.

Now I face total dependence upon Hank. It is sometimes

chafing, more often humiliating and belittling to be at his mercy; I am clinging to a hostile, noncaring force—like hanging onto an angry wind!

I am still prideful and this is one of the most difficult aspects of my panic. Pride keeps me, wisely or unwisely, from confiding in friends. Occasionally, the Bordens will say: "He's taking care of you, isn't he? He tells us he plans to be generous with you." Hank's dad also wants to be reassured that Hank is "accepting his responsibilities." I confine myself to short, wry remarks. Of course I have Alan, who nods sympathetically when I talk. He is my psychiatrist manqué. But even with Alan, I am squeamish about revealing what I know, what I think about Hank.

It is not so much the processes of law that I fear—though they are hardly weighted in my favor—it is Hank himself! The law, with its escape clauses, would allow Hank to pick up and settle in another state, thereby evading or at least postponing the financial demands of an estranged family. When I ask Alan what will happen if we do *not* reach an agreement, he replies: "You know the man better than I do. You're married to him!" Separation brings out the fear, so long dormant in the marriage, that Hank is no one to lean on. I'm afraid—literally afraid—of what he will do should I anger him, antagonize him, push him too far with my demands. My anxiety is fueled by my imagination. He will run away. He will quit working. He is a restless man, always seeking an unformulated goal, ruthless about cutting away what he no longer wants, no longer needs. There is no point in asking how the man I lived with, slept with, shared everything with, laughed with, held hands with, can now turn his back. Other men have done it. And it is my terrible suspicion that Hank could, too.

And now I am terrified at the prospect of being on my own

financially. I am trained, energetic, enterprising. I am all of these things, yet I know I am a financial dependent, one of the few dependencies I have ever allowed myself. I have earned money for long periods of time, but it has always been a matter of free will, of choice. Now I am facing self-support, not self-development! And I become more neurotic about money, not less.

I alternate between saving, for my peace of mind, and spending, to assure myself that things cannot be as drastic as I think. I will walk ten blocks to save a bus fare, but buy an expensive new outfit because, I rationalize, it is important to look well now. I watch nervously as each bill comes in, not certain when or how it will be paid, but I continue to incur new ones. I warn the girls that spending must be more "careful," but make every effort to keep our food, clothing, and small pleasures unaltered.

My attitudes toward money are educated and transformed by the economics of separation. I start out seeing myself as a financial drag on Hank, an inconvenience, but gradually I become more typical in my thinking. I'm "entitled" to support. Nevertheless, I want this aspect of separation to be neat and clean: surgery without blood. In due time, I become as much the outright antagonist as any other woman in my position.

The money is not only food, clothing, and the house in which I live; it is a more or less public coliseum where the disappointments, the angers, the desertion, and the revenge are played out. The lawyers enter, maneuvering, manipulating, moving, and feinting in a stylized parlor game they've played many times before.

The law, the economics of separation, and my anxiety converge in the agreement, which becomes the imaginary life line for which I must fight. It is through money and the law that I eventually learn I cannot react to Hank; I must take a stand of my own. He has an objective—separate existence—no longer part of "we," "us," "ours." He is moving within the immediacy of his own desires and interests, not thinking of coming back.

The amount of money to be in the agreement becomes the issue. "Fair" in Alan's lexicon is enough to maintain the standard to which I'm accustomed—for purposes of bargaining. Alan's task, as he sees it, is to bargain, threaten, negotiate the agreement as though he were making the best possible business deal. In the meanwhile, I am to continue living as I have been; I am *not* to take a job, not to manifest my capacity to support myself. But I do not understand Alan's arithmetic. How can one income, already pressed to support one household, now cover two? Doesn't something have to give way? I ask these inconvenient questions, touching reality for an instant or two—Hank's reality!

"Courts in our state, as in many states, award a wife no more than about a third of her husband's income after taxes," Alan explains. In practice, the provision is not as exact as an arithmetic table; the auxiliary benefits in Hank's business—the car, credit cards, membership in a dinner club and in a golf club—can be added on and considered "income," should the judge so decide. The trick on the part of the wife's lawyer is to appear before a judge who is a "family man," and a man who will take a jaundiced view of the businessman's many tax-free benefits.

Even as a novice in legal matters, I understand that going into court would be dirty pool and an all-out declaration of war. Alan mentions that he may subpoena the books of Hank's business in order to determine Hank's exact income and benefits. Even across the empty space between Hank and me, the prospect of angering him by so aggressive a move is unthinkable! I have spent my married life respecting the priorities of "the business"—the source of our livelihood has its own self-generating sanctity. "You're protecting Hank," protests Alan, "when it's my job to protect you."

I am not certain whether I'm protecting Hank or myself. I know only that I am reluctant to act, finally, as though we are enemies, or even to recognize that we are. I do not believe we will ever come to court. It takes the months that follow, clogged with negotiations and my own tortuous "progress," to bring me to the first step: "If Hank does not sign—yes, we will go into court!"

The lawyers begin the task of making separation legal, of arriving at an agreement. It is a slow, killing dance on a cold, dead ground. The smallest move takes weeks on a carefully prescribed route. The matter of the back bills goes through the process this way. Alan calls Hank's lawyer: "Before we sign an agreement, these back bills will have to be paid."

Hank's lawyer then tells Hank what Alan said. (According to the ethics, Alan can never deal directly with Hank, not even by so much as a simple telephone call.) With exquisite slow motion, the return trip then begins. Each call can take days, even weeks, to complete. Any one of the men in the triple play can be "out of town," "in court," "in a meeting." Sometimes true. Sometimes a simple method of outwaiting, outmaneuvering for position. But as I later learn, with each repetition—each "he said," "she said"—the original statement Hank or I may make is qualified—distorted, if you will—until, at fourth hand, it is misshapen, and cannot help but stir angers and resentments.

This accepted ritual, this tug of war, is all that seems left of the lives Hank and I spent together. In a movie about divorce, vintage enough to be seen on *The Late Show*, there is one scene that, for me, capsules the role of the lawyers. The estranged man and his wife are meeting with their respective lawyers to divide their property and sign an agreement. While the lawyers go down the list, assigning possessions, cutting the last threads, the man and his wife look on in consternation with what—if allowed to surface—would be regret. The lawyers turn their backs on whatever the clients may be feeling, turn to their own sociability.

HUSBAND'S LAWYER: You golf, don't you?

WIFE'S LAWYER: Certainly. Haven't I run into you out at Lawnview?

HUSBAND'S LAWYER: In a foursome with Milt Binzen! Great course, Lawnview. Dining room's pretty good, too. . . .

WIFE'S LAWYER: Ever try the steak tartare at Hillside?

HUSBAND'S LAWYER: Can't touch the lobster Louis at Lawnview.

WIFE'S LAWYER: Why don't we put a foursome together some weekend—eighteen holes and lunch?

When I saw this small scene in the movie, I thought that my last meeting with Hank in the breakfast room of our house had, for all its bitterness, been bitterness *with* each other. But now we had sicced the law on ourselves, and the law was pulling us apart, finally, inexorably.

CHAPTER V

Marriage on the Couch

*Fra moglie e marito non mettere il dito.**
—Italian Proverb

If women would sock away all that money instead of rushing to the analyst, they'd be independent when their husbands get restless . . .
—An eminent psychoanalyst,
off the record

AT THE low point in separation, I am helpless, bruised,
even terrorized. Nothing I'd observed, nothing I'd read,
prepared me for the total rout of separation, for the attack
on the daily structure of my life and, more frightening, on
the delicate balance of my inner vision of myself. Stripped of
self-esteem, I cannot even hide in the corners of custom and
habit. These are gone, and I am alone.

I turn to my psychiatrist: "How did this happen to *me?*"
It is less a question than a cry in the wilderness.

"You married the guy!"

I am shocked and angry as I drive home. Yet it may be

* Between a husband and wife, do not put a finger!

the most significant thing he has said to me in four years, this man who hands me his handkerchief, encourages me to cry, to go back to work, to play tennis; who gives me advice about Erika and Jill, about my finances, about what to say to my lawyer; this man who is my psychiatrist, my rabbi, and my friend. But this is his reality therapy, a reminder that outside of his office, where I talk freely, often sob, sometimes laugh, there is another world—the *real* world.

"You married the guy!" The words hang in my mind. I talk to them. Yes, I did marry him, and I must accept the consequences of my act. The harsh words free me, release questions, disruptive, disloyal questions I have tried to lock away. For ours has, at many critical points, been a marriage on the couch, where Hank and I each spent hundreds of hours, thousands of dollars; where we had four therapists between us. And now I must ask: Did psychiatry help our marriage?

I cannot afford the same detached judgment toward psychiatry that I have toward the law. The question is almost as hard to ask as it is to answer. My investment of myself is too great. Psychiatry is more mysterious in its ways, and, to me, more cowing in its authority than the law. But once I have the courage to be disloyal, to question, I range farther. Are the "sins of our fathers"—those forces put into motion by our childhood and our genes—subject to repair psychiatry? Can therapy carve happy endings out of the conflicting, often tragic forces of human interaction? Given any therapist's own inescapable human nature—his personality, his beliefs, what his grandmother used to tell him—in what direction will *he* influence a marriage? Can *any* psychiatrist buck the restless, dissatisfied climate that has built obsolescence into our human relations as well as into our manufactured products—an obsolescence that allows us to discard unwanted children, wives, and old people as casually as we cast off outmoded cars, ailing washing machines, and unfashionable furniture?

Ironically, what I have learned in therapy gives me the independence to question its authority. I also recognize that I am more subjective than objective, more a product of my woman's intuition than of my neuter capacity to reason. Hank would undoubtedly tell it differently, and each of the four psychiatrists involved tell it differently again.

I am the first to turn for help. The twins are five months old, and I am unaccountably agitated. I cry without reason behind a closed door. I drag through each day like a figure in a painful dream. I am ashamed to confide in Julia, who seems more at ease with domestic life, and characteristically, I am guilty because I *am* unhappy and upset. Jill and Erika are plump, cooing, responsive babies, albeit a double handful. Hank is bemused by the children's take-over of our lives. Yet the hard work and relatively "normal" tensions can hardly account for my state. I am not refreshed, even after a full night's sleep. One morning, with no prethought but the subliminal conditioning of our therapeutic society, I pick up the telephone and call Dr. Field, a noted psychiatrist. I take the first available appointment he can offer.

I walk out of Dr. Field's office in mild shock and call Hank to meet me for lunch. Dr. Field, I tell him, has said I must see a psychiatrist twice a week. Hank's response is instant and generous: "Of course!" I still feel a great warmth in the memory; he does not make me feel uncomfortable about the great cost, does not use the problem of money to cover his own fears about what psychiatry might bring about, especially between us. With untried faith, Hank thinks at the start, as do I, that help will make things better.

Therapy is neither as drastic nor as exotic as I expect; nothing perceptible happens in or out of the hours. I recall crises,

64

advice, recital, and repetition. The appointments are at 8:15 in the morning with Dr. Sari Caplan, a psychoanalyst of my own age, who lives only six minutes away—if I hurry. With two babies, my appointments take arranging. I am always rushing, always a few minutes late, appearing at the office in an old sweater and wraparound skirt—the precursor of blue jeans. Even Dr. Caplan, mild and uncritical, hints once that I may be a bit too casual in my dress. But Dr. Caplan's personality feeds the nondramatic and helps make my hours into a routine extension of my regular life, like French conversation class on Thursday evenings. She is a physically comfortable woman, with a quiet voice and no nervous mannerisms, who works mainly with children. She is redeemed from being the quintessence of Jewish motherhood by unexpected humor, a memory as astonishing as it is frightening, and a persistence in pursuing *her* point. She does not remind me of my mother.

I soon stop crying, take my tasks in hand once again, and come to the basic issue of therapy: myself. During my years with Dr. Caplan, I come to the well for help, albeit a subtle help that does not pronounce, but rather enables me to learn about myself. Implicit is the hope that sense and judgment will take over where my insights leave off. At other times, less pressed, without an immediate problem with Hank or the children to talk about, I empty my psychic trash can and begin to analyze my own inadequacies and fears, to examine the dammed-up resentment and guilt toward my own mother, which has direct bearing upon my need to prove myself a "good" mother to my own girls.

I discover the delicious luxury of saying exactly what I think, without holding back for the feelings, moods, temper, or desire of another human being—that is, when I can figure out what I am thinking and feeling! With Hank, who has fixed ideas about my role as a wife and mother, I try to respond as he expects. When the circuits get crossed, I can escape to Dr. Caplan's, where I test my reality against Hank's. The mixture of freedom and reassurance habituates me to help.

Psychiatry underscores what I already am: self-searching and introspective, slightly suspicious, probing for weakness in others as well as myself, and what my mother quaintly called me as I was growing up, "a freethinker." Another turn of mind enhanced by my analytic work is my search for the truth. I need answers. Absolutes. It is as though I could find in intellectual, rational certainty the sure affection and response I could not find in my original home.

"We'll have to stop now," Dr. Caplan invariably says at the forty-ninth minute. How many times, at that signal, do I gather up my pocketbook and coat and leave! I may be as unresolved as when I arrived or I may be on the verge of an astounding self-revelation. No matter. The hour is over. Many times I leave dissatisfied, carrying away the turmoil with which I came, a little accusative of Dr. Caplan because that day psychiatry does not work. But slowly, painstakingly we inch toward the core of the problem: the impairment of my sense of self.

The work is so personal, so much for me, that Hank figures only now and then. Undoubtedly I complain about him in the wearying way of married patients: "I said . . . then he said . . . and I . . ." But I hold tight to the assumption that, through the hours on the couch and my admission to the Promised Land of the emotions, Hank and I will work things out. Dr. Caplan tells me that "Hank has so much to give," but she also tells me that "in any marriage, it is the woman who gives at least sixty percent, if not more."

66

(I cannot help but wonder, with wry amusement, what a woman's consciousness-raising group would make of *that* statement!)

When Hank's moods become not only depressive, but oppressive and worrisome, I urge Hank to go for help of his own. I have Dr. Caplan's endorsement. Hank does go. He never discusses his hours with Dr. Bickel, his analyst, but he becomes fascinated with the theory and reads the major works in the field. It gives him another language and, as I teasingly tell him, a new hobby. He is now an amateur psychoanalyst. By contrast, I am insular, interested only in what psychiatry can teach me for myself. But Hank begins to recognize the underside of his feelings. He is sold on expressing feelings as a *suo bono*, while I am skeptical, wondering if expression alone will make for change, or merely give the mirage of relief. Hank becomes more open, not so ritualistic, not so conformist in his behavior, in his expectations of me. From signs and signals, I assume that in the privacy of his psychiatric hours he is attempting, as I am, to shore up his own image of himself. In this spiritual upswing, we set out for our year in Italy—perhaps to try out our new selves.

Six months after my return from Italy, Hank hits his rockiest time: depressed, panicked about money, sexually impotent. There is a series of "hotel" scenes in which he literally clings to me, demands more and more of me. We interact, as always. The more shaken Hank becomes, the more insecure I grow, and the less I can offer in calm, affection, understanding. I am afraid that the shelter he holds over me is emotional cardboard. I have no concrete evidence, no professional knowledge, but I begin to suspect that Hank is facing a nervous breakdown. With Dr. Caplan's encouragement, I call Dr. Bickel. May I come to see him? I am worried about Hank. Dr. Bickel's reply is orthodox psychiatry: "I'll have to talk it over with Hank."

Hank consents and we visit Dr. Bickel together. I hold back during our three-way session in Dr. Bickel's office. I am waiting for my time alone with Dr. Bickel; it is what I have come for. When Hank goes out, Dr. Bickel closes the door of his office, turns to me, and delivers his judgment, harsh and punitive: "You have no right to be here!"

"It is possible," he agrees, that Hank is having a mental breakdown. But there is absolutely no expression on Dr. Bickel's face as he speaks, no commitment to concern—and his posture is that of an unforgiving god. He does not choose to reassure me, to work with me in any way. The interview is over, a slap in the face, humiliating and guilt-provoking. I do not understand. Hank is in trouble; I am in trouble with him. But Dr. Bickel is saying to me, in essence, that he is Hank's ally, that I have my own analyst. Go to her! This is still the era of his-and-her psychiatrists; family therapy is not yet widely known.

Dr. Bickel sets me adrift with my fears. How can I depend upon Hank, who is afraid, who is incapable of handling his own existence? We slog through this period, as we do through other tense, unhappy times. I develop my own working thesis: hold on long enough, and this, too, shall pass. I never think seriously of leaving because I believe that wherever I go I will carry my problems with me, that the next place will have *its* anxieties. I think of our lives as built together—with unhappiness as part of the structure. But I am stubborn; I persist in thinking there is *more* to this psychiatry business, that there is still help to be had if only we can find the right combination, the right formula. Hank is now going to a second psychiatrist, and I say to Dr. Caplan, whom I now see only occasionally: "Perhaps I should go to a male psychiatrist—get another point of view." She approves and suggests Dr. Ben Diamond.

I find Dr. Diamond a heavy-boned, burly man with a sunny disposition, who in brief respites from the burden of his practice grows roses, plays championship table tennis, and barbecues the family steak. He is even-tempered, pragmatic, quick-thinking, with confidence in his own powers. He could as easily be a businessman as a psychiatrist—a genial, very successful businessman. He is even relaxed enough to yawn in my face when he is tired, to look slightly bored before he says "Get to the point, Eve." He is quick to make judgments, tougher than Dr. Caplan. From the start, we are on a first-name basis.

I turn to Ben just in time. I am coming into another turbulent time with Hank. His total acceptance of me, which has been the cornerstone of the marriage, its real hold on me, turns inside out. Hank becomes bitterly critical, hammering away at his insistence that I must change. Change! A demand. An ultimatum. I become defensive, as always. What am I doing wrong? Is Hank right? Do I need to change? And yet, in my own thinking, change is still a riddle, a conundrum. I simply do not know whether people can change, particularly at our ages. Oh, I know the devices. Subdue part of one's self. Pretend. But these are not true changes. They are stand-ins, and can become unbearable and costly, as I well know.

I dog it out, turn to my research work, spending even weekend hours at my office desk, and I find satisfaction in my small successes. I use what I earn for travel. I combine my work with running the house, driving Erika and Jill to and from their many afterschool "advantages"; I give and go to dinner parties, play tennis. I am always busy.

Then there is Paris. And the illness, which I acknowledge as *my* form of breakdown, even though it is largely physical in its manifestations. During the dreary, desperate months in the hospital, Ben Diamond comes often, spoons out chicken soup when I am too weak to sit up, holds my hand in his, pushes the damp hair back from my forehead when I am feverish, restless. He teaches me how to breathe when I think I am suffocating with the illness and the drugs. He stands by when the accumulation of drugs and the illness itself drive me momentarily out of my mind. When the schizophrenic episode is over, Ben helps me to see that all of my life I have been afraid, that I am still the child afraid of the terrible shouting, the doors slamming, afraid of the echo of violence that crackled in the air of my parents' house. Ben helps me fight back against one overpowering nurse who is a bully, teaches me isometric exercises even before I can take my first steps down the hall, helps me fight to a full recovery.

I am not as clear in my mind about Ben's role in the period immediately before and after separation. For a brief period when I am most destitute of emotional warmth in my life at home, I think—in classic patient style—that I am falling in love with Ben. He is warm and personal, tells me openly that I am an attractive woman. "I'd be interested myself," he says more than once, "but you're my patient." I take this as one of his small jokes, although I make sure never to appear in *his* office in an old sweater and wrap-around skirt! We become good friends. We admire each other; we kiss when we meet. I know that he is friendly toward everyone, but I think he is especially friendly toward me. The closeness has its drawbacks. I am loath to be angry or openly critical with Ben. I am always polite, friendly, so that I am, ridiculously, hiding occasional shame, pride, irrational hope, or childishness from my own psychiatrist!

His warmth does not extend to Hank. I cannot escape the suspicion that he neither likes nor trusts Hank. He tells me, more than once, that Hank is selfish, rigid, self-seeking. Only a few weeks before my illness gets out of hand, Hank and I come to Ben's office together. It is my last effort to break the deadlock of Hank's accusation against me, and my passionate self-justifications to him.

I do not know what I expect the day I take Hank to *my* sanctuary. Perhaps I expect Ben to do battle for me, to champion my cause. But Ben is at his most matter-of-fact, quieter than usual. Nothing that day is easy and funny, as it often is between us. With Hank present, even Ben's jokes sound unfunny. The discussion soon focuses on the matter of oral sex, which Hank prefers and I do not. Hank says I am "ungiving." I mask my discomfort in talking about sex openly with a super poise, a fake physical and mental calm, while Hank lounges back in his chair with his air of "I will not. And nobody can make me!" Ben does not pressure Hank. He simply asks him questions while I sit quietly by. But the fifty minutes are soon over and nothing has been defined or decided. Afterward, Ben says: "Hank's rigid. He's not about to give way!" But Ben is for me and does not pretend otherwise. I need and want his support. But it must be faced: what is good for me is not equally good for Hank. I cannot help but ask: Is this the meeting with Dr. Bickel in reverse?

Like that meeting several years earlier, this one is a total flop. We find no magic, no alchemy to make a golden peace out of the dross of our misery. Hank tries, actually, in the following weeks to be more considerate of my viewpoint in spite of his show of defiance at Ben's. By then, however, so much else is wrong. I am sick at heart, discouraged by fulminating failure. I think wearily that we cannot start afresh, not in marriage—with or without psychiatry. We are victims of our years of living together and, going back even farther, of the original imprinting in the homes of our childhoods.

When the last impasse comes, Ben does not counsel me to stay or to leave. Although he has already said that I am trying to keep an invalid marriage alive, he now tells me: "I do not want to preside at the breakup of a marriage."

It is, it must be, *my* decision. And in making that decision, I must accept whichever seems the greater reality to me: what the therapist is telling me or my intricate relationship with Hank.

"Can you live alone?" Ben asks, and in the bitterness of the moment, I reply with maudlin rhetoric: "I'm alone now!"

When Hank announces that he is leaving, Ben advises: "Let him go. When a man wants to leave, nothing can stop him. He'll be back."

Once Hank and I are physically separated, I can no longer tell myself that psychiatry will change us, will make things better. I am very skeptical now, and a little bitter about help. But I must have somewhere to turn. At first, I am resistant, too proud to go. I make an appointment with Ben only when I am most frantic, in dire need of someone to listen, someone to advise me. Sometimes I think that for all our friendship, Ben doesn't "dig" me, that he is too matter-of-fact, perhaps *too* well adjusted himself.

We have one meaningful fragment of dialogue that leaves me particularly unsatisfied. I am self-accusative and raw to the touch the day I tell him: "I have failed in the central relationship of my life."

"*Was* it the central relationship, Eve?" His negative is spelled out in his voice, in his shrug. I back down for a moment. Then I think: "He doesn't understand. It *should* have been. I wanted it to be. I tried to make it so. Ben misses the stress in my sentence; it is not the relationship, but my failure on which I am hung up."

Often I envision our psychiatrists as seconds in a battle, egging each of us on to win for ourselves. I entertain the image that not two, but four, of us are in the marriage: Dr. Bickel perching on Hank's shoulder, telling him how he should feel, what he should say; Ben, whispering in *my* ear, counseling; while Hank and I are talking, quarreling, making love. We are too sophisticated to act out the travesty of "my analyst says," rebutted by "*my* analyst says," but our seconds stay with us, nevertheless. Psychiatry, like the law, does not create our adversary situation, but somehow accentuates it.

On balance, I know that therapy works for me. I have sobbed, laughed, gathered enough new strength to go on. But I have a strong gut reaction that in our case, therapy is divisive for the marriage. In those seductive hours, so purely for *me*, the interaction with a thoughtful, detached (and paid) human being is necessarily different from my interaction with Hank, who is not only less reasonable by make-up, but less reasonable by dint of his role: he is my husband! While I consciously strive to be truthful in my analytic hours, whatever I say is my part of the truth; what Hank tells his psychiatrist, what he arrives at, is *his* portion of the truth. Each of us clings for security, for self-confidence, to his own truth.

And so I come back, like a round, to the question of

whether psychiatry is a luxury that taxes the marriage rather than contributes to it—but I am a product of the therapeutic society. I still wonder what oracle, what guru, what new formula for living we might have missed. I am in the habit of help.

CHAPTER VI

Wicked August

All that once hurt . . . goes on hurting in new
ways . . .

—DENISE LEVERTOV

AUGUST IS a slothful month, waiting for September to
signal a new year. I have never liked August. This one is
wicked. I am scattered, inattentive. Lack of joy edges my
thoughts, a grim border to each day. I recite my new litany
of envy, and dislike myself for envying others. I become a
selective magnet, attracting whatever makes me question
myself, whatever provides fresh fodder for my unhappiness.

I live through my own spin-off of the Sisyphus myth.
Awake, I roll the stone uphill, fighting against a devalued
view of myself. At night, while I sleep, my conscious efforts
and controls turned off, the stone rolls back down. In the
morning I must begin the struggle again, from the bottom.

One day, alone in the house, I act out my own psycho-
drama. I play the part of the rejected woman. Hank's bank
statement arrives in the morning mail. He has yet to change
his mailing address. I want to take that as a sign that he

cannot move out altogether, but I know too well it is simply Hank's way. He hates details. I stare at the envelope; then like some character I half remember from a novel or a play, I steam open the envelope and go through Hank's checks. I hardly know what I expect to learn, but I find out how much rent Hank is paying, that he has bought a bed, two chairs and an air conditioner. I do not learn how he feels about his new life; I do not learn whether he ever thinks about me.

I am caught! I cannot reseal the envelope properly. It looks tampered with. Like any child in consternation over his wrongdoing, I hide the evidence. When Jill says "Daddy wants his new bank statement," I shake my head and complete the act: "No—I haven't seen it." The envelope is still hidden in a shoe box at the back of my closet.

Blessedly, the thick August heat moves out. The air becomes cool and fresh. My body releases its defensive discomfort. I stride along, stirring with thought and energy. I am cheerful. I think wryly: "Another life experience! This will test what I'm made of." I think: "It will be a challenge, excitement, drama—perhaps an opportunity. Well, I'm exaggerating. At least it will be a new experience."

My mood doesn't last long—there is a message at home: "Call Alan Springer."

"Hank's lawyer," Alan tells me, "has brought up something we have not discussed yet: divorce. Hank wants a divorce." Divorce! Not so soon! I have simply not come that far. Naïvely, almost childishly, in these first months of separation, I literally do not consider divorce. I do not move far past the struggle and conflict of our last days at home, past the Now. Divorce is for "someday" when I might want to remarry, when Hank meets someone. But this is sooner than someday.

Alan is still talking, but I miss several sentences because

my pulses are pounding. I have a sick headache. My buoyant step forward is short-lived. "Hank says of course he has grounds!" Grounds in our state are still limited to adultery and desertion.

"That's ridiculous," I reply. I have assured Alan from the start that I have not committed infidelity. But "of course he has grounds" stirs memories that testify against me, not at the visible level, only at the level where things are not what they seem, a hopelessly deep, enmeshed level where affection, respect, mutuality wither and die.

I have deserted, not in the eyes of the law, but through disloyalty, lack of faith, my inability to love Hank as a husband deserves to be loved, those uncommitted acts that violate the pact between a man and a woman more than atrocious behaviors.

Infidelity? I take no satisfaction in the letter of my fidelity. Not that I would be naïve enough to chide myself for doing my share of smiling over drinks, engaging in provocative conversations, for I am more tease than intention, seeking admiration and desire from other men, but withdrawing quickly when I arouse a response! I am unfaithful in a far more dangerous way; in the tenderest, most intimate moments, I hold a part of me stranger to Hank, a secret self saved for my dreams of a man who might someday, one day, come along, if only in a brief encounter. In my forties, I still dream of being aroused and fulfilled by a faceless Prince Charming.

Alan has been talking all along. I hear him say: "He must have another woman." I am carried so far into my own thoughts, I almost miss his point: if Hank wants a divorce, it must be because he has someone else!

In fact, he does. And classically, I am the last to know. I cannot ask my friends to tell me who she is. I will not ask Julia, or question Erika and Jill. When the girls come back from their evening with Hank, I ask my usual question: "How's Daddy?"

"He's fine." And we discuss what they ate for dinner.

But Erika and Jill know. My friends know. "He's been involved for quite a while," John Borden feels freed to tell me, once *he* knows that *I* know there's a woman. "He has a new household. He wants to start a new life. He wants a divorce."

I make wild guesses about who the woman could be, guesses that prove imaginative, and wrong. Erika finally gives me an inkling, once I calmly mention that I know of the woman's existence. "Yeah," Erika tells me, "we had dinner at the apartment this week, and Leslie baby made us meat loaf." Leslie: the name of a television actress, a divorcee, Hank was seeing when he and I first met. I make an easy guess this time: he has gone back to her.

I do not totally understand myself. If I do not love Hank enough—as I have so long thought—why am I now so rankled, so shaken because he has another woman? Do I love him because he's out of reach? Because I'm possessive? Is this a lesson in primitive jealousy, in the full meaning of "my man"? Afterward, when I meet a large, buxom woman of sixty who says about her large, dull husband: "I never let him out of my sight—a good man is hard to find," I do not think it such a big ha-ha. In the world of women and men, I finally learn, the woman must hold onto the man she has— or scramble hard for a new one.

I tell myself many sensible things in the next weeks. I am

a good lecturer—if only my emotions will listen. I tell myself every look backward is a waste of time, a prolonged burial service; that self-study is self-defeating, that it breaks down the power to exist, saps vitality; that waiting, wearily, to reach a safe harbor of serenity is a pitiful joke; that crises, surprises, problems go on without end as long as we are alive. That I have only one thing: myself. My capacity to be, to enjoy, to give where giving is needed and wanted. I tell myself to cry, to finish the task of unhappiness, then go about my business.

But how do you put away a pain you did not suspect, could not have guessed, would be so great?

I am strict with myself, censor my daydream that Hank will tire of the woman, that he will remember and need me, that he will come back. But I cannot so easily control my nighttime dreams, in which Hank returns, in which my problems are over. In these dreams, I am comfortable and at ease. In the morning light, I know instantly that I am a fool, that there is every evidence it is over, that Hank has left as fully as a man can leave.

As an antidote to dreaming, I try remembering how it was our last months together, how alone I was, how unprotected, unsheltered in the angry atmosphere. I remember what I wanted most: to be freed from Hank's sullenness, his coldness. Now I am free—if only I can free myself!

"What have you done? You've changed everything!" Geraldine exclaims. Hank's bed is gone, the bedroom rearranged. On an impulse the week before, I called a decorator, a close friend who had lived through divorce herself. "I've always wanted a monklike bedroom—spare, empty, serene," I instructed her. We agreed that the rug must come up, the floor be stained and waxed, and gauzy white curtains be hung at the windows so I can see the trees through a soft haze. The room redone takes on the unmistakable look of a retreat for one. The girls stop in when they come home from school but make no comment. It is clear: I no longer expect Hank back.

What is not visible—or clear—are the batches of Hank's clothes and possessions neatly stacked in a corner of my closet. I hold back from throwing them out, or from shipping them down to his apartment as a defiant gesture. Nor do I give his bed away. I hide it in the storage closet. I'm not sure why. I do not spell it out for myself.

I wait anxiously, impatiently, for the end of August, for the time to go down to the small beach house we rent, year after year, at the quiet end of a quiet island. We call it Formica Palace, in deference to the owner's taste in decorating. But it is *our* place. We come back to watch the gulls wheel over the marshes, to ride our bikes along roads bordered by bulrushes, to loll in the sun, to exclaim in "oh's" and "ah's" each evening over the orange sunsets.

I love the stop in time, the total nothingness, as much as anything in the pattern of my life. The long stretch of empty beach is my private Lourdes; here, walking along the hardpacked sand, I have always sought and found myself. "Here," I think, "will be the place to find the sense and serenity to keep me going."

We have rain. For three days and three nights. Not a soft, benign summer rain, but an angry beating down that makes us all captive to one another and to the restlessness endemic to seashore houses in the rain. At last, when the rain stops, I can go down to my beach where I have walked so often before in thought, in hope, in turmoil.

This time I have a sense of task; I have the resolve of

80

desperation. *I* know how slender my controls are, how close I am to cracking. I have to find my way, have to change. It is Hank's dictum to me, updated to meet the new circumstances. How does a woman in her forties—with physical and psychic scars, with the brand of failure—how does that woman change, retool—for what?

My mind will not respond to command. It slides off into corners, hides, tries to escape. I walk long hours along the water's edge while the gulls circle for food in the tangle of seaweed washed up by the storm. I have no sense of my own movement, no recognition of getting tired. I am aware only that my mind is spinning where it will. No one is more surprised than I at what it now offers me: not answers to my preoccupation with a future, but a sudden, unbidden look backward into the years with Hank, into myself, with an understanding that has eluded me not for months but for years.

With the clarity of a religious revelation, I see what, in my defensiveness, my self-protection, I have failed heretofore to see. Lying deeply hidden beneath my efforts to be a conscientious wife and mother, my good manners, other people's portraits of me—even the mirror of myself held up by two psychiatrists—I see what has been there all along: that no one, anywhere, at any time, has been as good to me as Hank.

He has offered me a share of everything he had. Above all, he offered himself. He wanted to share his love, in and out of bed, his worldly goods, his enthusiasms, his worries. He offered me a view of myself as a wonderful woman. I never wanted him to think otherwise, yet I thought: "He's a fool to be taken in by me. I'm *not* wonderful." I took all that he offered as my due, while looking upon his gifts with criticism and suspicion. If he worried when I went out alone at night, if he was protective, I called it "neurotic." I failed to pick

81

up my ears, failed to hear the friend who said "I wish *mine* would worry." I had what she wanted. But I was aware only that I found it restraining and chafing.

I often thought of Hank as weak, a pejorative word that builds up an accretion of disrespect; as though with a label, I could wipe out the confusing infinity of detail that keeps me from achieving total insight and understanding of another human being—even my own husband!

For years I had been telling myself that it was I who made the concessions, made the effort to "get along." But under the ceiling of the somber, grayed sky, I stumble on important recognitions: I have been acting out of fear, out of guilt. I'm not that damned "good." I'm a huge cover-up. My attitude must have penetrated the marriage in a thousand small gestures and expressions—in the very air between us. Within this framework, I can see that Hank may have been acting not so much out of aggression and hostility, but *re*-acting to the part of me hiding from myself and from two psychiatrists!

Why did I fight Hank's affection, concern, genuine caring? I fought being too well loved as much as I now fight not being loved at all. I am incapable of moving far enough from myself; the center is still in such turmoil that I must fight off friend and enemy alike. I am never certain that I can go to my own inner storehouse and find what I need: love for myself, or another. Or just plain adequacy.

Under the spell of the waves washing hypnotically back and forth at my feet, I see that Hank was offering much that was good, much that was not, but that it is my nature to dwell on what is weak and insecure. I cannot love and give where there is not perfection, strength, superiority. I do not stop to ask myself: Why would a strong, perfect, superior man need *me*? Hank is neurotic, anxious; he is held back

from expressing much within him. But hasn't my nonacceptance fed into his problems, magnified them? By overlooking
what he did offer, didn't I stress what he could not?

I have been trapped, in spite of my intentions, in the
pattern of my own parents' lives. I have been feeling
"superior" to Hank, without realizing it, just as my mother
felt superior to my father. My father was the legendary young
boy who sold newspapers on the corner, who carried the
money home so his family could buy food. He never went
past the second grade. He did not have time! My mother,
who came from a more prosperous middle-class family with
bourgeois pretensions, studied to become a teacher. It was
part of her folklore that my father was beneath her socially;
my grandmother, my mother told me many times, had
opposed the marriage with a "crude" man. But my father
was also handsome, dashing, virile—if uneducated. My
mother wanted him. She had to have him. And in the marriage, it was his virility, his masculineness against which she
fought, against which she foundered.

What was different about my "superiority" to Hank? I was
attracted by his sweetness, his thoughtfulness, his view of
me, but once these belonged to me, I could only devalue
them, search for something else.

When I strip away the protective covering, I am sorry.
So sorry for hurting Hank, for failing him. I can no longer
afford to be angry for what he has done. I, too, have done
much. It *is* true, as I told Alan Springer so glibly, no one is
innocent in a marriage. Hank *does* have grounds.

I think: "Now I have lost everything! Lost it as surely as
though I had thrown it away: affection, respect, protection—
all, for so many reasons I did not understand, did not want to
know until now."

I cry new tears. But what, after that, do I do with the self-knowledge? Ironically, it brings more self-knowledge. I admit what I have not been able to admit these past months. I do want Hank back; Hank, not simply the marriage and its setting.

CHAPTER VII

Encounter

The tears of the world are a constant quantity.
For each one who begins to weep, somewhere
else another stops. . . .
—SAMUEL BECKETT

W H E N W E leave for home the next day, I am oddly elated. What can I *do* with this sudden knowledge of myself, so much like a birth brought forth only after trauma and labor? I hug it to me: a secret source of purpose and strength. It excites me. But there is common sense. There are facts. Hank wanted to leave. He is now living with another woman. He has his own self-inspiring revelations!

I pile the sandy towels on the floor of the laundry room, open the week's mail, put the house to rights—then stretch out in my monastic bedroom and study the play of light on the whitewashed ceiling. I try reading the Sunday newspaper, try shutting off the imaginary dialogue in my mind, slowing down the beat of my heart. Suddenly it occurs to me: ask Hank to come back! Tell him you're sorry. I have not the slightest concern with pride or saving face.

But Hank, the girls tell me, is leaving for California that

day. I cannot wait a week to call him, to ask him for Sunday breakfast, to tell him what I am saying soundlessly to myself. Why not call? See if he is still at the apartment. I scramble through the papers on my desk with impatient hands, looking for a note from Hank that says "Here is my new number in case of emergency." I have never used it.

I dial. "The number you have reached is a wrong number. Please dial again." The voice in the recording mouths each syllable.

I dial right the second time. "Hello." I hear Hank's familiar voice. It's a nice voice. Responsive. Inviting.

"I want to see you."

"Yes, of course. Is anything wrong? Are the children all right?"—responses I know so well.

"Yes, yes. The girls are fine. When are you leaving?"

"At five o'clock. I can come up, if you like—"

"No, Erika and Jill are around. I can come down—"

"No, I don't think that would be a good idea."

"I didn't mean to your apartment!" I smile. I am still *that* normal. Imagine my seeing Hank with the "other woman" sitting there!

"How about my office?"

"Good. It will take me about forty minutes."

I find a tranquilizer, look into the mirror and am grateful that my skin is tanned, my eyes almost black with my eagerness, my hair soft and becoming. I dress too hastily for my hands, which are stone-cold, clumsy. But I feel confident in a new burnt-orange dress. I look well.

I give the car too much gas as I back out of the driveway, the car bucks, and I must wrench the wheel with a sharp turn. There are so many cars out on the street—each one is in my way.

I don't have to think hard about what to say to Hank. I

find the words easily, in my preview: "I want you back, as a friend, a husband, a lover." I pray as I drive, how I pray, that he will be receptive. I think of coming home and telling Erika and Jill: "It's going to be all right. Daddy is coming back." Of calling my mother. "It's all right. Hank is back." I even consider how we'll start going out again with friends, how casually I'll make the announcement: "We're together again." I try to hold back, to keep my mind from racing ahead of the car. Only habit keeps me from going through red lights, from making dangerous moves as I drive along the crowded highway. I smell something burning. "Someone has bad brakes," I think. But no! It's me! Not now, not car trouble now! Then I look down: I am driving sixty miles an hour with the emergency brake on.

There is no parking space in town. I have to walk four blocks from a garage in my new shoes. I'm slowed down. I must wait for the elevator. Each small obstacle endangers my self-control, my self-possession, as brittle and fine as spun glass.

The elevator operator stands by suspiciously as I ring Hank's office bell. "It's open. The boss is in." I walk past the Herman Miller receptionist's desk, the collage over the couch that Hank and I bought at the Whitney Museum, the hand-designed rug with the company's insignia—the status symbols I once shared as the boss's wife.

Hank walks down the hall to meet me. So much the same, but fresh to my eyes after the past months. And suddenly dear. He is wearing the tweed jacket we picked out together, but the slacks do not quite "go" with it, and he's still wearing his old loafers, run-down at the heels.

"I need a drink to say what I have to say," I tell Hank, even before I sit down. He is gracious and finds a bottle of Scotch in his partner's desk.

Hank sits in his deep leather swivel chair behind his desk. The Boss. The setting supports him, gives him status. But he is the gentleman. He is poised. He is Hank at his best, conducting a difficult interview, handling himself magnificently. And it hurts.

"No, it isn't hard—it's simple. I want you to come back. I need you—as a friend, as a husband, as a lover." I say it directly, just as I said it to myself in the car. But I wonder now: "Does it sound overdramatized?"

Hank answers my proposal: "No. I won't do that."

For me, the meeting is at an end. I should go. But I cannot leave. There is a fascination, a warmth in being there, even in the terrible circumstances. We talk a short while. I am calm. I do not cry, although I feel a few tears that I coax back. I smile, and try to lighten the moment. I *know* I am playing the scene for everything within me. I want sympathy, but not too much sympathy, because I want to remain an attractive, desirable woman in his eyes. My voice stays well modulated, but it takes the same gargantuan effort I must make when I speak on a public platform.

Hank is open. "I gave you plenty of signals. You're good at reading signals. You're a damned smart woman. Where were you all those months? Where were you a year ago?"

"A year ago I was just getting out of the hospital."

"I didn't mean that exactly. I know where you were. I was there."

I am actor and onlooker in the scene, part of me already withdrawn for protection. Anything I say or do will be useless. Why am I churning up what is old and past? Why am I walking over hot coals? Hank has so much anger, and he is justifying himself. He echoes the last month at home, but, strangely, does not antagonize me. He is dissolving my fantasies.

Hank invites me to continue talking: "If you have anything to say, I will be glad to listen. . . . When you got beyond my neurosis, what did you tell yourself were the reasons I left?"

I can see no point. He does not want me. Yet I am touched when he says, "I know it took courage for you to come. I know what it must have taken. I've lived with you. I know you have your pride."

Perhaps I should have cried, should have poured out my confession of guilt, my new knowledge of myself. Reason, intuition, my sense, hold me back. My timing and his timing do not jibe and the opportunity is lost.

"Are you happier?" I ask.

"Yes, I'm happier. I did not like the life I led. I want you to know that there were no women before I left. I didn't go sneaking out behind your back. I did not leave for another woman."

I don't think he looks *that* happy! He doesn't look cared for. His hair is shaggy, his socks the wrong color. His office is a mess. I think of the burned-out matches, newspapers, pipe tobacco, shoes—everywhere and anywhere at home.

As we walk out to the elevator, I ask if he'd like a ride to the airport. No, he's ordered a taxi already.

The togetherness is gone by the time we reach the street floor. Only an old silence between us.

"Now I know. Now I know . . . it's over," I am saying to myself as we ride down.

We say good-by at the corner. I look directly at Hank. "Don't be completely taken in by my act. It's costing me dearly." He waits to hear more, but I do not know what I can say, little short of pleading, and I will not do that. I wish afterward that I had kissed him good-by.

On the way home, I am not crumpled and weepy but

almost buoyed up. For one thing, I am reminded of Hank's terrible anger, so strong it is almost a physical force. Strangely, I do not remember *my* hurt and anger, only Hank's. But that day his shortcomings cannot aggress against me. They are his own. I can even smile because he looks sloppy, and think musingly, "That's the way he is. He's afraid of life, but life *is* fearsome." I see marriage, as I could not when I was in it, as a being together, as a paradoxical, impossible combination of letting each other alone, while offering one's self to the other. It all seems clearer to me—after the fact.

I do not have the smallest concern about losing face with Hank. The stiff-necked, protective pride that has so long been my defense against hurt—sometimes a hurt more imagined than real—has been more of a burden to me than anything Hank has ever said or done. I am suddenly free of it. Or I think, this minute, that I am free. I did what I went to do. No psychiatrist guided me, advised me. No one served as the midwife for my emotions. Hank did not respond as I imagined or wanted him to, but I have yet to be sorry.

I am freed by the encounter to look backward with less self-punishment. Yes, we did have much that was good together; affection, growth, an everyday solidity and support for each of us, along with the strain, cross-purposes, dissatisfactions. I did not stay because I was a fool or a craven coward. I am released from the steel trap of my own thinking.

CHAPTER VIII

A Small Memory

In someone else's fond embrace
I'll close my eyes and see your face . . .
—POPULAR SONG

EARLY AUTUMN. I was born in September and have always loved those weeks when the light is uncompromisingly bright and golden and the sun—though higher—will still warm me at my center. The bees drone, but are heavy with oncoming cold; the harvest of early apples, green peppers, eggplant, and tomatoes is piled into supermarket bins, posing for a Renaissance still life. The earth's cycle is fulfilling itself. The weather no longer invites one's ease, but bespeaks purpose and activity. The girls are back at school; the routines are in force. I accept a new work assignment, the first since separation. I enroll in two courses at adult school: mythology and folk dancing. I play the piano for the first time in many months.

The separation is becoming itself, forcing acceptance, accommodation; breaking in finally on the "I" of me. I can no longer put off deciding whether to repair the cranky old washing machine or to buy a new one; I can no longer treat

Erika and Jill as figures in a familiar landscape. Like the washing machine, they force my attention. They are restless now with my prolonged drama. Erika joins a small theater group and uses it as a pretext for staying out until two in the morning. I roil with fear and anger, and lie waiting for her return. Our confrontation is stormy and useless; she is skittish, scornful, riding roughshod over my authority— "Who asked you to wait up!" Later, she confesses to a teacher who befriends her: "I always thought my mother was so strong! I was testing her." Jill talks with Hank on the telephone as though this were the best of all possible worlds. I am amused, surprised to hear how seductive her tone is. But I know she is spending more and more time alone in her room, building her fortress of denial.

I meet the next hurdle: a raw, acute loneliness. Always there, always threatening, if I do not plan ahead. I grab at any place to be, anyone to be with. I must be with people; yet with them, I continue to be alone—a touch of insanity, the alienation of unhappiness. Now I know what the woman meant when she asked me, months earlier, "How do you handle the loneliness?"

But I will not be suppliant, not for pity, not for friendship, not for money. I reach out where I find life good-humored and accepting. But I am proud and—I hope—sensible. I know that I cannot fasten onto other lives like some barnacle. I can only touch them lightly in passing—an evening, a dinner, a day's outing—even if I must become the Little Match Girl outside in the cold, looking into the warm, lighted living rooms of other lives.

Who will fill the void? Not my friends, not our children, who have been raised with so few demands, not Ben Diamond in my occasional hours. My need is simple and deep: a man. I tell myself that it is not sleeping with a man I need so much as the male companionship. The woman in me is bereft.

John Borden offers to be my brother; he means nothing more by it. "I am still Hank's friend, but I'm going to help you." I accept the "help" with charm and graciousness. Small things: financial advice, a visit with me to the lawyer, who resents John's presence. After a few weeks, I drop the new relationship. John is content. He has made his gesture, just as each of us, in someone else's crisis, will make a generous gesture or two. We are less generous by habit.

I am invited to join a friend and her husband for a quiet dinner at a local restaurant. A movie afterward. I go once. Twice. But no more. Never more than twice with any woman and her husband. I remember hearing John Borden complain, before it applied to me: "I hate taking an extra woman to dinner."

I join three women for our usual Sunday tennis game. But they must scatter early. One left Sam alone, watching the football game, and must get back; another is having company for dinner; and the third explains that "Harold says since I'm working, I'd better stay home weekends and clean the house." I no longer have these obligations. I am free. Free to do as I please. To have opinions without the censorship of caution or of wisdom. Why is the freedom now harder to handle than the obligations against which I once balked?

I am brave enough to go to my first large party alone. It's a wedding reception with an assorted crowd, not the selected, concerned group of friends who have been holding out an umbrella of sympathy to shelter and protect me. I have walked into a roomful of people many times by myself, with only the most casual explanation: "Hank's in California this week" or "He's at a chess tournament," then settled down to enjoy the evening. Hank's presence as a husband was an implicit framework. But tonight I walk into the room on guard: against curiosity, against intrusion on a painful privacy. I have checked my appearance carefully; I am dressed well, but not too conspicuously, not too stylishly; enough make-up to withstand the fluorescent lights, not enough to look too brave! I fervently hope that my *bella figura* will be in my smile, in my voice.

"Your husband's not here either, I see." I turn toward the handsome, brittle woman whose voice is shrill with her particular unhappiness. She asks, "Where is he?"

"Gone with the wind!" My response is instant and inane. I had not checked over my dialogue beforehand. Later when I walk to the parking lot alone, I am mighty sorry for myself, but also impatient. I recognize that the allowable time for suffering is running out.

I am convinced that the self-searching on the beach and my encounter with Hank have produced seismic movement within me, that I have touched bottom and *want* to come back. Slowly, slowly, the shift begins to evidence itself in small quasi incidents.

At a dinner party, I walk into a bedroom and find Ceil Hoffman, a woman of sixty, married thirty-seven turbulent years to a man who enjoys other women, crying bitterly: "I never should have married him. It was a mistake!" A scene both comic and sad; yet I see at that moment the woman's unending capacity to suffer, and I am reminded that I, too, am a skillful sufferer.

I open a magazine on the train and read a personal-experience story that, on the surface, has nothing to do with my life. I read with the relevance of a punch to the jaw; "The capacity to withdraw from the relationship will be the measure of my future."

I am ready for change, looking for change. I play a small game: I try breaking some of my most entrenched habits. I walk in a different direction with my poodle; I eat something new for breakfast; I try a new perfume—called Futur! I begin to think of practical matters, and decide I should remain in the house for another year and a half, until the girls are graduated from high school.

I am sitting at my desk trying to plan my new assignment when the telephone rings. "Dr. Slawson is calling," a well-trained, but indifferent voice informs me. It is Cal Slawson, an Abraham Lincoln–looking man, an even more successful surgeon than he had planned to be, married to Minna, whose bleached hair and birdlike movements camouflage her brains and clout. Cal wants to know how I'm managing. And would I like to have dinner with him that evening—"Minna's in Cleveland visiting her mother." I accept, delighted to get out of my own kitchen, out of my own small orbit. "Put on your best dress and look your prettiest. I'll pick you up at six-thirty." He promises to flirt outrageously. Cal has always liked his small jokes.

I look forward all day to having Cal's ear; he's brighter than most men I know, hardheaded, and prejudiced in my favor. Perhaps he can advise me on the snag in my legal affairs with Hank.

That evening I go from emotional rags to riches.

We are halfway through our first martini when Cal announces "That's enough of Hank." I have a feeble reaction: I should be more protective, more loyal to Hank. We've been four-way friends for more than ten years.

But I am enjoying myself far too much. To sit opposite this vigorous, attractive, and literate man is a shot of adrenalin. It is a relief in itself not to be the extra woman, the woman markedly without a man! Even the way a man holds your coat, opens the car door, shares the menu, is different when you are one woman, not part of a group. (In my circumstances, two women constitute a "group.")

Cal is attentive and gallant beyond the call of friendship, but he's always been courtly and courting with women. Nothing to take too seriously. To me it is history, not current affairs, that Cal once confessed he was in love with me. At the time I turned it aside with a smile and a "thank you," meaning "no thank you." I assumed that in the midst of our continuing four-way friendship that so small a pebble had quietly settled at the bottom of the pond.

By the second martini, the evening has a direction of its own, distinctly different from the one I had in mind. Cal is openly admiring. And I am not loath. As dinner progresses, I can feel that we are enjoying each other, regardless of the words or the subjects. We talk about Cal's work because it is an overriding part of his life. I do not have to act the part of a good listener. I am totally absorbed.

We drift into more personal talk, about what gives Cal his total absorption in medicine, and whether it will always seem worth the take-over of his life. We talk about children—his and mine—and about me. I am captivated, though not convinced, by his view of me as a vibrant, intelligent woman —not yet knowing who I am. Soap-opera talk, but hard to resist. Besides, I am surprised. Cal has always seemed so much the important, successful doctor that I did not think he could find time to observe others about him—including me. At this level of intimacy, away from party talk, away from the accepted manners and social observances within our foursome, he has a sweetness and sensitivity that are deeply appealing.

I am dwelling on the beginnings of that evening because I did not consciously suspect where it was leading. Not until the second drink did I fully realize that the carefully circumscribed friendship was out; we were a man and a woman exploring each other over the table with our words, with our eyes. I do not eat more than a mouthful of the filet mignon. I am far hungrier for the admiration, for the acceptance Cal is offering. I am suffused with pleasure, the martinis, the moment. Inside, a visceral warmth I have not felt in a long time. I am being aroused. I think: "For God's sake, the sex thing is catching up with you, Eve!" I am not scolding or chiding, just telling myself.

The evening has a simplicity and momentum; there are no small awkwardnesses. "May I kiss you?" Cal asks when we are back in the dark car. I smile. I want him to; if he did not, I would have been stranded in my seat, my senses pounding and wanting. His kisses are warm and fresh; I kiss him as a desirable woman, desiring, my whole body responding. It is easy and good to have a man's arms around me again, not in habit, not in anger, but wanting me.

Cal asks if I will go to a motel with him. I answer as a woman aroused, no feints—except the one reluctance I force myself to speak about: that I am sensitive because of the surgical scars of recent years. "I will make love passionately, tenderly to the essence, to the woman you are." He puts me at ease.

On the ride to the motel, he holds my hand; and that is almost as much consummation as I need: to feel wanted, cared for. We take each other's measure in verbal banter, the words as much a part of the intercourse as bodily contact. No, he tells me, I am not too much woman for him.

He is not afraid; he knows he can dominate me. It is a delightful game, to play for sexual power with a man who is intrigued, not afraid that I am too much for him sexually.

Until that moment, I did not quite know how these "casual affairs" happen or are handled except in books and movies. I wonder, in the silent minutes as we approach the motel, whether Cal is having second thoughts. I will not let mine surface. I think defiantly: "It is a game I can play because I am free, because I am beholden to no one." All along, though, I know I'm showing Hank! I do not consider Minna. She literally does not exist for me that night.

Only once before have I walked into a hotel with a man other than Hank, intending to go to bed. It was the summer I finished graduate school. Ancient history, predating the sexual revolution! At the time, it was the most daring act of my life; retroactively, it is dated, an old-fashioned memento, like a shirred satin garter.

That night as I drive up to the motel with Cal, I am, in fact, living dangerously. I am vulnerable on every possible score; not the least is my legal status as a separated woman, still without a financial agreement signed. Cal, very married, has as much to lose as I do.

He suggests that I give him a head start, then follow him to the room. I am superbly poised, for me, as Cal unzips my dress and turns down the bed. Ridiculously, after living in a nonprudish marriage, I can find it unsettling to see a man other than Hank slip out of his trousers, then out of his shorts. The martinis and the warm impulses are faltering. But I do not want to leave. I am curious, compelled to get into bed with a man other than Hank.

For an aggressive man, Cal is a sensitive, provocative lover. I do not think for more than an instant about the strangeness, about my scars. I accept his caresses, respond passionately, easily, without pretense, without self-consciousness. My body is in tune with his.

It is not a satisfying sex experience for me; it is a warm, human encounter. The newness, anticlimax—I'm not sure what—makes Cal tentative. He says he is inhibited because neither of us is using contraceptives. But it puts me at ease to find that he is not a mechanical expert, a seasoned Don Juan; and it throws me back to the many times Hank thought he would not be able to complete the act. I am incredibly naïve for a woman of my age and my living, but in my "salad days," Masters and Johnson had not yet revealed all about sexual adequacy. I think simply: "Even stronger-seeming men than Hank can be unsure of sexual climax." I remember the old saying: "In a second marriage, there are four in the bed." Not *exactly* applicable, but applicable enough. I miss Hank's ways; I wish that the arms were his, not a stranger's.

Cal shakes his head afterward as we sit up against the pillows, smoking and talking. "You're a psychological virgin!" I know he's right; it is ludicrous to be waiting still, at my age, to be completely aroused and fulfilled.

We must leave the warm, comfortable bed so Cal can take me home. I am composed, released, and astounded by what I have done. Cal walks out to the car first. Calmly, with more nerves than brains, at 2:30 A.M., I walk through the motel lobby to Cal's car.

In my own bed, I hug myself like a sixteen-year-old who has newly discovered the excitement of her body. What will it be? One evening? Cal talked of "our getting used to each other." I am awake a long while in pleasurable thought, but the next morning I am up as early as usual. My eyes are shining like stars. Someone will guess.

"Who'd you have dinner with?" Erika calls out from the bathroom.

"Cal," I reply, as casually as I can.

"Cal?" she echoes, with worldly questions in her sixteen-year-old voice.

"It's all right." I laugh to make it so. "Minna suggested it!"

Champion guilt maker that I am, it is astonishing that I do not feel genuine guilt about that evening. It was its own moment. Isolated. It is only later, when I sometimes envy Minna Cal *as a husband*, that I feel uncomfortable. Wanting Cal that night seemed natural, not immoral. Perhaps it is true that morality is more a matter of circumstance than of convictions.

I am half relieved, half disappointed that Cal does not call and invite me again. Whenever we meet, he flirts outrageously, and far too visibly for my comfort; he encourages me to call him. I do not. Yet I would kiss him now, if he were here, and thank him for that night. In the weeks that follow, it serves as a small memory with which to warm myself. The days ahead are cold and ugly.

CHAPTER IX

What Do You Do About Sex?

Sex is so good for the complexion!
—Tallulah Bankhead

''What do you do about sex?'' The woman who asks
the question is telling me, obliquely, why *she* remains in her
own unhappy marriage. I do not answer her question; it's
none of her business. But I must ask and answer it for myself.

The episode with Cal, which fleshes out my daydream of
an attractive man finding me desirable, also invites compari-
son with what I have known. Looking back, I am not surprised to find that the sex between Hank and me was better
than either of us recognized. I do not believe we were only
"used to each other," which can be a hiding place for a
woman, a trap for a man. I believe we fit together in basic
animal desire, in our chemistry, that what went wrong was
in our heads. It seems clear now; the interference, the static,
came from our thoughts, our words, not from the direct, intuitive responses of our bodies. We took our troubles *to* the
bed. They did not originate there.

It goes back to our honeymoon, in the land of winter
sports, which proved to be a mistake for Hank. "I'm afraid

I won't be enough for you," Hank says on the first night. The power of an idea! He is not realistic. He *is* a good lover; he can lead me easily. He does not have to be a sexual athlete for me. I am relatively inexperienced, and have waited almost too long. My sexuality has hardly been sleeping; it has been racing within me till now, causing a conflict of body and conscience I cannot resolve. I can neither abstain nor "go all the way." I am neither truly virginal nor truly experienced when I meet Hank. But I am twenty-five and custom and conscience can no longer hold back my woman's body. We drift into a sexual relationship. It is easy enough. I am living away from home, working, in another city. I permit myself a sexual freedom that I think is long overdue. I do as I wish, with guilt the important spice. But I worry. Then, as later, Hank is a thoughtful lover and teacher. But I am not at ease with the situation. At first, it seems novel and daring, but I come to see it as an aside. I want to marry, to get on with my "real life." I want to marry Hank.

Significantly, only when we are married does Hank worry about his sexuality, just as I worry afterward whether I love him enough to be married to him. We are asking far more of ourselves than we did in the casual affair. This is the ultimate: this is marriage. It has to be "right." It has to be "good." We invoke romantic, impossible standards because now we are committed.

On my honeymoon night, I go into the bathroom and cry. What have I done? It's a mistake, a terrible mistake. And Hank's concern about sex and his ineptitude at skiing are idiotically mingled. It is to be the first of many times that Hank's inadequacy will cause me to panic. I do not face up to my own shortcomings: that I do not have the compassion, the understanding, the surety of self to reassure Hank. Nor do I have the simple knowledge that many men, as well endowed by nature and appetite as Hank, have similar fears of failure.

On my side of the bed, I am strongly sexed, a powerhouse of sense and reaction, which has its benefits and drawbacks for a man like Hank. But I have not come to terms with my strong sexuality. I am bound by conventions more suitable to my mother's generation; I do not truly know how to let myself go. Still living in the shadow of the puritan tradition, I am ashamed to reveal either my need or the extent of my sensual response to Hank's caresses, to his almost too successful stimulation of me. Hank's expressed fear of his inadequacy now holds me back even farther.

But we are young. And sexed. And often we are carried along by the natural need and rhythm of our bodies, our appetites more powerful than our problems. Nature has her own strength and wisdom.

I cherish the time in bed, as a woman will, as an act of human closeness, a breakdown of the barriers we build during the day by our manners, our activities, the battery of small defenses and avoidances. More often than not, Hank and I seek each other out without too many words, take from each other what we need, give what we can. I do not achieve the abandon of a mill dolly and Hank is still judging his own performance harshly, but we are satisfied more than we are dissatisfied. The hours *after* lovemaking are, for me, the true intimacy; I need to be held close against Hank's body, to be at rest in the quiet dark, and talk out of the depth of myself. Here, in these hours, is the core of marriage, what keeps it going through a flood of daily demands and crises.

I awake happy and serene after a night of sex and its

deeper aftermath. I have renewed warmth, buoyancy, will, for whatever comes in that day. I cannot look upon an orgasm as a physical experience alone; it releases more than tension in the sexual organs. It releases the person within, for me always a benevolent release of well-being, feeding my flow of affection and kindness toward everyone, everything around me, including the dog and the cat! Even the nights that are not "successful" are nights of giving and taking, of mutuality.

But we take our troubles to the bed; the soft, gentle moments, almost evanescent, must needs counterbalance cross-purposes, pressures, economic worries, and illnesses in our "other" life. It is a delicate balance between us that holds—until that last year, when the problems become so outsize that they assault the nerves, the senses and impulses needed for intercourse; and the angers, so runaway that they take the place of sex itself.

Hank grows outrightly dissatisfied with me in bed, and says so, many times. "Loosen up, for Christ's sake," he will tell me, just as I begin to lose myself in the act. I grow tense and self-conscious. The sex becomes a problem: a narrow problem. Hank quarrels with me over what I should do in bed— what I think I *cannot* do: that is, to accept oral sex as a totally fulfilling act. I consider his demand "unmanly," weak, arbitrary; it seems to me he is regressing when he makes foreplay the entire sex act. I have either simple ideas or simple needs. Only the final act of intercourse, the primeval sensation of a man within me, gives me satisfaction. How much of this is bodily wisdom? How much of my viewpoint is my training translated into words, which cannot be trusted to convey the entire experience? Sometimes I go along because I am pleased with Hank, pleased with myself that day.

But at other times, when I am pressed, unhappy, or at low ebb, I do not have the margin to give; I cannot make myself do as he wishes, and it becomes a matter of conflict. Hank's insistence makes it an obligation upon me, not a volitional act. I cannot find out whether it *does* or *could* bring me pleasure.

Hank is annoyed because I tend to be "straight," to resist sexual sophistication, to cling to the testimony of my own senses. He has another complaint: I am not aggressive enough. He never truly understands, in all those years, that though I seem so energetic, so self-motivated and self-sufficient by day, I am feminine and leadable in bed, in the soft receiving dark. Everything within me cries out for a passive role. He complains. We quarrel. And he strikes where I am vulnerable—at my vision of myself as a desirable woman.

I have other memories that fill out the picture, that make our sexual experience, like the relationship itself, hard to describe as "good" or "bad." Hank not only makes demands; he is deeply responsible as a sexual partner, eager to please and satisfy me. I have never failed to understand and be touched by this, even when I am in conflict about Hank himself. One night I am more outspoken than usual. I tell him he deprives me of pleasure, makes me tense when he announces as we begin to make love: "I don't know if I can make it tonight." He never says that particular thing again.

Undoubtedly my illness and surgery take a toll of my confidence. As a very young woman I had a vanity and narcissism about my body that I would never dare admit to a living soul. It was a beautiful, shapely body—and I knew it. Even through many years of marriage, it remained a young woman's body. But mutilation and scars corrode vanity. I can face down the world during the day, clothed; but in bed with a man, I cannot muster confidence, or the ability to talk and make light of what troubles me. I am ashamed of the changes, and hiding the shame. Hank is a great gentleman; he protests that none of this matters to him, and I want to believe him. I half *expect* him to be enthralled, half *fear* he will no longer be. Almost until the end, our long knowledge of each other, our many nights, stand behind us; we can still find each other, briefly, in a sexual encounter, and be carried along together by the sensuality and warmth it engenders. The moments grow fewer. And finally none. I do not sleep with Hank in the last months.

I come back to the practical problem facing me as a woman alone: What do I do about sex? The answer has to be: literally nothing. The very term "sex"—depersonalizing, mechanistic, isolated from any involvement with the personality of a specific man—does not exist in my vocabulary of experience. I do not think myself capable of sufficient pragmatism—call it flexibility—to take "sex" like a meal for which I am hungry.

What will happen in my aloneness, in my exclusion from male company, I ask Ben. He asks me, in turn, if I do not realize that women often turn to autosexuality. How uninformed can I be, a woman in my forties? I literally do not understand him at first. He means masturbation! Self-stimulation. I find it hard to admit either to myself or to Ben that during the long months of illness I occasionally surprised myself into self-stimulation. I was not only uncomfortable with the idea—I was not good at the performance! Or, to be more precise, I did not find it satisfying. Hank, with his knowledge of my body and responses, can please me so much more than I can please myself!

I am left with sublimations; an absorption in my daily life: work, children, housekeeping, the weekly sets of tennis.

And the hope that by nighttime the day will have been so long that neither my body nor my mind will trap me. In the tense, agitated time, I do not think much about sex as an isolated act. I am too discontinuous, too jagged to know how bereft I am. Sex, for me, is fundamentally a healthy appetite.

Part Three

The Business
of Separation

CHAPTER X

Negotiations Begin

It is not a bad thing to have to face total failure.
It toughens the spirit and makes one aware that,
though all may seem lost, human beings have un-
quenchable resources within them.

—MAY SARTON

"H o w ' s y o u r Latin?" John Borden asks me.

"Weak."

"Remember the phrase *'amicus curiae'*—friend of the court?"

This telephone call from John will beget telephone calls that will beget still other calls, as well as meetings, and a bitter-tasting encounter with Hank. We are being forced out of our private shadow play of feelings into the more public drama of money.

"Look, Eve, Julia and I think this lawyer bit is a travesty. It could go on for months, and cost thousands of dollars. Why not pick a neutral third party and let him work out the agreement? A kind of friendly conspiracy? It will save Hank lawyers' fees and taxes. Hank is willing. And you have nothing to lose." John then cautions me not to discuss this with Alan Springer. "We don't need him."

My instinctive response is a No. It feels wrong. I do not enjoy having "nothing to lose." I don't *want* to save money for Hank. And I am being asked to by-pass the only person absolutely, unequivocally for *me*—Alan Springer, who, acting in my behalf, does not have to be "reasonable" or "impartial." And yet I have a terrible clarity about money that is produced by tension, fear, and my wild imaginings. I do not want to be recalcitrant, to appear hardheaded and grasping—an outright, predatory bitch. I am clinging still to the possibility that, in time, Hank will come back. Three months, and the relationship with the other woman will fall apart; his anger toward me will abate. He'll miss me. He'll change his mind. I do not know how he can be so cool; how, after twenty years, he can pull out and I cannot.

John is waiting for his answer. I do not want to declare open warfare, to slam the door with finality on any lead to a reconciliation with Hank. Yet John's suggestion sounds more like conciliation than reconciliation. I must protect myself financially *in case*—in case I am to be a woman alone for the rest of my life.

I must come to a stop somewhere. John is still waiting for my reply. I try to sound level and thoughtful: "Let me think about it." We agree to talk it over at my house that evening.

John's last word to me is "Don't be too emotional!"

"That's pretty funny!" I reply, but John has already hung up. Of course I am too emotional. It's the unavoidable trap, the end product of months of stress. That's why one wife, when she's left, will call all of "their" friends and ask for help in getting her husband back, and another will tell De Sade stories about her own sexual relations with her husband. Doesn't John remember how emotional *he* was when he came to tell me of Julia's first affair?

John tells me he is "my" friend as well as Hank's and I believe he thinks he's being fair, but I sense that he is acting for Hank through an unavoidable identification. John, too, is a husband; and he, too, may have to meet the financial demands of an erstwhile wife. Besides, John is a businessman; he can look upon my marriage as a bad deal, to be dissolved as expediently as possible, without guilt, without recriminations.

I do not know how to back away from John's proposition, but I must. I do not want to be in the position of presenting "my case" to a neutral third party, who will undoubtedly turn out to be still another mutual friend. In these circumstances, I cannot fight for myself; nor can I sit quietly by and let Hank "take care of" me. What I say, how I act at each juncture, now becomes critical. I find no macabre relish in the excitement, as I know some women do, no delight in being at the center of this troubled stage. I have no talent for strategy or tactics. Yet I cannot accept others talking, planning, scheming for me, dictating my lines, writing my scenario.

That evening I must justify myself, prove that I am reasonable as I sit with John and Julia in the familiar setting of my own living room. "Maybe I am overreacting. But I want to carry this off with dignity," I confess. I am really speaking to Julia, who protested to me that morning on the telephone: "How can I know what's going on if you don't tell me?" She is hurt and puzzled by my steady withdrawal from friendship in the past months. She cannot understand how her "objectivity" could possibly antagonize me; it seems so right, so loyal, to her.

I phrase the next with picked words, hoping to expunge the trauma, the tears, the hours of self-examination. "I want to leave the door open."

But I *am* revealing myself because John says instantly; "He won't come back!"

"You don't know that, John," Julia breaks in, "you don't know what can happen in a year."

John shrugs. It is his most characteristic gesture, almost his attitude toward life. Influenced, as always, by Julia's opinion, he adds, "Well, Hank did say he neither needed or wanted a divorce right now."

The relief is so great that I am suddenly high-humored, almost happy. Casually, John is telling me the most important news of the evening: I do not have to face divorce! At least not yet. The relief from pressure is so intoxicating that I reveal more than I intend. I tell Julia and John of my fear that Hank might pull out, sell his share of the business, and move to another state. Julia nods. Yes, she, too, suspects this is possible. Instantly, I am afraid my revelation will backfire. I urge them to be discreet; particularly Julia, who, in her openness, releases confidences at the wrong time, like balloons escaping their moorings. Even a hint to Hank that I am afraid he might run away could, in itself, give him a subtle permission to do so.

John suggests that, as the first step, he and I meet with Hank. Neither Julia nor John guesses from my composure that the prospect of sitting down with Hank is both fascinating and unbearable. I have not seen him since the Sunday in his office. I hold onto the crazy hope that by meeting together, a sense of belonging, of obligation—even of history—might be fanned into being. Julia wants to come to the preliminary meeting. She says; "I have more influence with Hank than anybody."

"No—just John, *if* we have the meeting!" Julia, for all her sensitivity and insight, does not see what she is declaring: that she has inherited my influence with Hank! I do not want a woman present who now has my role, even if she is supposedly using it in my behalf.

The next morning I stand in a hot shower long enough to induce a preternatural calm. I want to see Hank. I want to match my frantic fantasies to a real human being. I hurry out of the shower, still warm and damp, wrapped in a towel. I sit on the edge of my unmade bed and dial John's office number.

"I'll do it. Bring Hank here for breakfast on Sunday."

I am buoyed up by playing a role in my own life. I call Alan and instruct him to hold off on any further negotiations with Hank's lawyer. Alan is patient and noncommittal. He gives me only the mildest of warnings: that it is not advisable to have other people in the picture. "I've never seen a matter settled that way."

But I already have my others involved. That afternoon I have an appointment with Ben Diamond. I literally carry my fright, my total confusion in my hands. For the first time in all these months, I have thought of suicide! I have not let the thought go far, but its emergence, even for a moment, is frightening enough. Ben thinks it is healthful that the thought has surfaced. I report the details of my meeting with John and Julia. It is more of a legal than a psychiatric matter, but I want his opinion: Is it wise, I ask, to put the Bordens in the role of intermediaries?

"Don't talk to Julia," Ben tells me. "She's not disloyal, but she's unwise in where and when she talks. She'll do more harm than good." He's said all this to me before, but until now I have fought accepting it.

"I've let it go too far to call it off now," I say helplessly.

Ben is pragmatic, as always. "Then look your most attractive on Sunday—and a little helpless."

Does he think there's any possibility of Hank's coming

back? "Forget it!" he answers crisply. "Hank's finished with you. You're cut up. He's not coming back. He's free. He's got someone else he wants. He'll be happier so long as she caters to him, so long as nothing happens. But in the end he'll run true to form.

"Hank is a man who can walk away completely, leaving you stranded. In time, he can walk out on the kids, too, if necessary. That's his way of handling conflict and guilt; to deny it, turn his back on it. He's done it before; he can do it again."

By chance, Friday is Yom Kippur Eve, the most sacred holiday in my religion. The Kol Nidre service, always beautiful and hallowed by suffering, seems particularly significant that evening. As I sit through the service with Erika on my one side, Jill on the other, I read the silent devotion: "Forgive the iniquities of others against you, as you would have God forgive yours . . ." The words are directed at *me*, advising *me*. The girls, too, are released by the service. Jill cries, and I touch her hand; then Erika cries too, and I put my hand over hers. We are still standing at our seats at the final prayer; the congregation is already moving slowly up the aisles toward the doors. I am slowed down by my thoughts. Suddenly I announce to the girls: "I'm going to call Daddy and ask him to come back." The woman ahead of us turns around, unable to contain her curiosity. She is in time to see Erika, taller than I, hugging me with a rib-crushing hug, her head down on my shoulder, sobbing "Oh, Mommy; oh, Mommy," while Jill looks on, more composed, but her eyes shining with the hope that "all this" will soon be over.

When we get out to our car, I find a chain blocking our exit from the "friendly, adjacent parking lot." I am so tense, so eager to get home and call Hank that I have no patience in reaching a solution; I drive out the back way—straight over a cement block. There is a loud crunching noise. We ride home with a broken muffler dragging and rattling.

Hank is not at his apartment when I call, but the switchboard takes a message. More or less appeased, now that I have acted, I go to bed.

"Is anything wrong?" It is midnight when Hank returns my call. Even in my semi-awake state, his anxiety sounds familiar. No, I assure him, my voice high and tight with excitement. "We have just come from services, and we want you to come back."

"Now is not the time to discuss it."

"Is there somebody with you?" Obviously a wrong question. But then, I do not know that the "other woman" has literally moved into the apartment with her clothes, furniture, casserole dishes and spice shelf!

"Not now. We'll discuss it on Sunday." That's all Hank will say.

I am insistent. "But John will be here."

"After John leaves." His dismissal is final.

By Saturday I am apprehensive about the plan for Sunday. I certainly do not want to discuss money with Hank. I've known that from the start. I call John and change the arrangements. "*You* discuss the money with Hank. *You* carry the message to Garcia."

"But what about the breakfast on Sunday?" John asks. I suggest that Hank can come alone and talk with me.

What I do next has no sensible explanation, unless you realize that the world is crowded within my head: a weary, beset, frightened head.

I call Hank and ask if, in honor of the holiday, he'd like to take the girls and me out to dinner that night.

"No." Hank is curt and cold. "And there's no point in my coming tomorrow. I'm not coming back."

Thud. I hold out for his coming anyhow, my voice controlled, my words cajoling in a constrained way.

He protests. "I don't want to say bitter things."

I press. "But we should talk. It's better than silence."

"All right," he says finally. But there is no promise in the acceptance. No willingness to listen. I cannot undo the telephone call; I have called him so many times, I can't call him again and tell him *not* to come.

Hank comes ten minutes early, and he is a Hank I can dislike and be bitter about.

The breakfast room is polished, gleaming, and filled with flowers. The sunshine is bright in the newly washed windows. I serve my best breakfast: fresh strawberries in orange juice; blueberry pancakes with bacon; strong hot coffee. I follow Ben's instructions and dress in a soft yellow blouse and a long orange skirt. My voice is low and quiet, amost a church hush.

I speak first. "Do not turn your back lightly on all this, on being wanted. Try to sort out what is anger at me, what is anger at life. We have had good and bad, but we have had it together."

Hank's face is closed against me. He does not hear me, although his response is reasonable. "I have no desire to make you unhappy. In many ways, you are a fine and wonderful woman"—he is describing me, I think, as one of those excellent, antiseptic women who will never tempt a man to seduce her—"but I am better off where I am."

The conversation is out of my hands. I have nowhere else to go.

But Hank does. He brings up money, and I think suspiciously: "That's what he really came to talk about."

"Don't fight me," he warns, "or I'll do everything in my

power against you. I'm going to take care of you"—there it is again!—"but I won't be pushed."

I try to mollify him, to modify the anger, the stony coldness. "We could hardly make it financially when we were together. With two households, it's going to be hard."

"Remember that," he says. Not kindly. "If you go after me, I promise I will bring the wrath of the gods down on your head." He reminds me, needlessly, of his skill in this area, and he adds, "Nobody is going to tell *me* how to spend my money!"

This is not the Hank I conjured out of memory as I walked along the beach; not the Hank who is firm, yet sympathetic, sitting at his own desk. This is the man who could not bear to be within our four walls in those last months, the man I could no longer live with. This is the man who could be ruthless when he was through. I had watched Hank discard a business partner after ten years, without a qualm; watched him move away from old friends without the small pangs that one experiences at the end of a friendship. And most significant of all, I saw him grow angry and bitter toward his own mother as he went deeply into his psychoanalysis; he became as cool and contemptuous of her as he is now of me. I think: "I should have known I could be next. Would be next." I didn't believe it possible.

When Hank leaves, I go out to play my Sunday tennis game. As I serve, I hear Hank again. "Don't fight me, or I'll do everything in my power against you."

On that Sunday, I have seen Hank close to being evil, certainly malevolent. Yet in my dreams I am still rescuing the Hank who smiles, laughs, and goes eagerly to bed with me. My waking mind is trying to move on, but my sleeping mind is still rescuing the disaster.

CHAPTER XI

... And More Negotiations

This is a world of chance, free will, and necessity—all interweavingly working together as one. Chance by turn rules either and has the last featuring blow at events.

—HERMAN MELVILLE

AFTER THE Sunday breakfast with Hank, it is—as he was wont to say—a whole new ball game. With negotiations no longer influenced by my thinking that Hank may be back, it becomes more critical than ever for us to reach and sign the financial agreement. I cannot afford to by-pass Alan's protection, but how can I stop the wheels I've set in motion; stop the "friendly" proceedings with Julia, John, and Hank?

It is Monday morning. If I call Alan to countermand the instructions I gave on Friday, I will sound foolish and indecisive, the protoype of the hysterical, stranded wife. Yet I need advice more than ever. Hank's threats do not sound to me like the typical saber rattling of a husband protecting his money. To me, they are a measure of Hank's capacity to be unreasoning, to make an unpredictable move. I am afraid!

"Lenore Coleman!" I say it aloud. My "eureka!" Why

didn't I think of her before? Lenore is a friend, as well as an outstanding lawyer who works in the civil-rights movement, not in the acrimonious field of marital law. But perhaps she will advise me. When I call, she points out that there is a problem of ethics: I'm another lawyer's client. But she senses my urgency, and out of friendship agrees to see me as a one-time thing.

She does not pooh-pooh my concern as overreaction. She states the problem in the first five minutes. "If Hank wants to pull out, there is absolutely nothing you can do. You are at his mercy. He has all the trump cards.

"There's no justice in this. We're the worst state of the Union in this matter," she tells me. "Hank can get a divorce in another state. So long as he doesn't return here, that divorce will be valid. And he will not be obligated to pay you a cent!"

What about my going into our county court for a support order?

"If he doesn't *want* to pay what you are awarded, you may have to be back in court every other week. Your lawyer will have to go through proceedings each time. The expenses will grow. You'll be in the middle."

Lenore gives concrete advice. "Sell your house, get a job, cut back, take whatever Hank will give. That's all you can be sure of getting—what he agrees to give. Under no circumstance should you give Hank a divorce! If he wants to settle for a hundred thousand dollars it would not be worth it for you to give up Blue Cross, Blue Shield, and major medical insurance. That is your first need. Then comes the children's college education. Get these essentials in writing—then take whatever he'll give. Add to it by your earnings. That's all there is open to you. If you push him, you'll get nothing.

"Affection runs downhill," she adds as a personal commentary. "When a man first leaves, he's eager to do the 'right thing' for his wife and family. As time goes by, he feels less and less obligated. Less and less involved." She is giving me the lesson I have already learned: that we are influenced by where we are—and with whom.

Her final advice is: "Get the Bordens out of the picture. Call your lawyer. Tell *him* to sit down with Hank and Hank's lawyer—without you. It's done that way. Let them figure out something. Now. No more delays. Tell them all this is the advice of your doctors, that the situation is making you ill."

I move on Lenore's hard-boiled advice. The next morning I report to Alan that "Hank is getting nasty."

"I've heard the same threats many times before," Alan tells me. He is neither impressed nor concerned. "I don't know any man who carries them out."

I am confronted with a study in two lawyers: Alan and Lenore have diametrically opposite viewpoints. Alan is putting his chips on the law and its processes; Lenore sees Hank as a man capable of side-stepping the law. During the events of the weekend, I wanted to play a role in my life. Now I *must* do so. It is up to me to act upon one viewpoint or the other, to choose my "poison."

"I can't bear any more of this," I tell Alan. "I am being pulled in too many directions. It's making me physically ill. I want *you* to sit down with Hank and his lawyer. Do what you can—without me."

Julia calls when I am trying to calm myself, to allay panic. She knows instantly—she's a bright one! "What can I do? I'm calling to see how you are. What do you want me to do? If you want me not to see Hank again, I'll do that."

Strange. When she offers, I cannot accept. I feel deserted, betrayed by her, but I cannot take away Hank's only real friend. On Sunday I allowed myself the fleeting wish that

Hank were dead—as though that would resolve my problem! But he isn't dead. He's alive, and confiding in Julia. "I listen—I only listen," Julia once insisted to me. "I don't talk at all." But Hank needs her, and I am apparently still attuned to his needs, no matter how alone and resentful I may be.

My guard is down. I need help. I need sympathy. And at the minute, I am compelled to talk. "I'm desperate," I tell Julia. "I don't know where to turn—and I'm getting sick again."

"Sick" is what does it. I embellish a bit. Give the main symptom: blood—the signal that my old illness is reactivated. Julia is alarmed.

"Blood! Something must be done. This has to stop. I'm going to call John right away."

I have finally screamed for help, and somebody has heard me. Julia calls back in ten minutes. "John and I will be over tonight. Hank's coming, too. He wants you to know he is deeply touched by your illness. He wants to straighten things out."

I do not respond eagerly. I had not expected this. "No," I tell Julia, "it's more than I can handle." And I am being honest.

Julia urges me to go through the evening. "Hank is in a placating humor."

I go along reluctantly. I am still close to the Sunday meeting in the breakfast room. But now I have action. My adult school class is at seven that evening. I go in spite of all that is ahead of me. I sit in class, inattentive, taut. When I get home, the Bordens are driving up with Hank.

Lenore, running the show like a figure hidden behind a screen, has pinpointed the one technique I have been too proud, too "real" to use, although it occurred to me long before she suggested it. After my long illness, any threat of recurrence would be an obvious bid for sympathy and attention. But the emergency could prove more real than fictitious if I do not get ahold of myself.

I *know* that Hank is particularly vulnerable to illness. It is his pattern. As a child, he saw his father take better care of, and more interest in, a sick wife than a well one. Hank's dad, a handsome, dignified, lonely man, was devoted and thoughtful when his wife was ill; when she was well, he could not abide her.

"This must be settled tonight," Julia announces as she walks in. They have ridden around the block several times before coming in. Julia is in charge of the evening. John leaves the talking up to her. Hank, too, is quiet, overly polite in the awkwardness of meeting after Sunday. In a whispered aside, Julia informs me that she is urging Hank to return; perhaps on a basis that will allow each of us more freedom.

The four of us sit in the same room where we have played so many word games, discussed so many problems, laughed—and quarreled. The lamplight is still golden on the dark wooden walls; the bits of silver and copper I've collected have a sheen in the shadowed areas. We are stiff in our chairs tonight, and purposeful. Yet I sense that this may be a bridge back.

Julia is forcing Hank's hand—toward me. He and she discuss how much money I will need each month. They arrive at a sum and Julia asks whether I think it a fair amount.

After my talk with Lenore, it sounds to me like a lifetime of security, a fortune each month. It is agreed that the sum will cover everything *but* my medical bills and the girls' spending and clothing allowance. John makes a small speech: I must try to be careful, to keep close track of my expenditures. Like a compliant child in an authoritarian second-grade classroom, I agree to try.

Hank brings up the subject of the back bills. He has every intention of paying them, he tells me. The note about *not* paying them was dictated to him by his lawyer. Hank says, "I have every intention of being honest, decent, and fair—and I mean it!"

As he says it, I think: "He does mean it. This is different from Sunday." I milk his words for something more: not money to live on, but the chance that he might be willing to come back. Hank is still talking in his slow, overexplanatory way, but I am not impatient. He is open and warm with me, not bitter and shut away as he was on Sunday. I do not listen to his words—but to the feeling.

I remember, now, that Ben Diamond once said to me, "I don't think you like the guy!" When Hank is like this, I am moved toward him, delighted by him. Ben does not understand the mixture of resentment and discontent with affection and involvement. Ben is simpler, not so fluid in his emotions. Not so neurotic.

"Do you have any questions? Ask any questions you want," Hank tells me. He repeats it. I come out of my daydream and ask Julia and John to go into the kitchen. I suggest that they hunt in the refrigerator for a snack—"That will keep you both busy." When I am alone with Hank, I have only one question: I ask if he will come back. I act compulsively, as though I do not know how *not* to ask him.

"I can't answer that now. I'll leave the door open." Then he makes an odd proposition that I never do understand: if I am well in two months, he will come home for weekends, starting with the holidays in December. He'll see if we can work something out.

Will he take me out to dinner in the meantime?

No, he doesn't think so. He's not ready. I drop the matter, and nod that I understand, which I don't.

But now I have Hank's promise of a fixed sum per month. I know someone in the room ought to say "Put this in writing," to make it legal. It cannot be me. The reality of the law will have to be set aside; I am negotiating for more than a monthly check. I cannot allow a particle of distrust to surface. Anyway, I think practically, an agreement that Hank makes voluntarily will be more honored than one that is forced upon him.

We have run out of drama, emotion, words. There is a brief discussion of doctors; of my seeing the specialist. Then Hank says that if I have no more questions, he will leave. I watch him walk out of his own house to go to his downtown apartment, and I wonder: "Will he be back?"

I have no more feelings left. I take a brandy and sleep through the night. When I awake in the morning I am emotionally black and blue. Exhausted. I have fought with everything I can use. Whenever I seek my own ends, I am not at ease. I tell myself that it is not "my way." But if it works, who is to naysay it—except my own conscience?

I have a new bone to worry and gnaw over: how will weekends work out? How will it be, coming together with Hank again after all that has happened? And what has changed from those last angry months when Hank was at home?

CHAPTER XII

Sex and the Social Scientist

. . . all wives are faithless
all women are wanton
—WILLIAM CONGREVE

"BROWNING? You've been seeing *him?*" Ben Diamond is surprised and amused. Raoul Browning, a psychologist of international reputation, has recently arrived at the research center in our suburb. He is known for his original thinking in the field, his charisma as a lecturer—and for womanizing. Ben warns me: "Browning has broken hearts from coast to coast." I nod. I know. And Ben is content that I will be sensible about Raoul Browning.

I do not even *try* to be sensible. Knowing him sets free a great covey of birds in me which fly high and far. I am infatuated, enthralled. Without intellectualizing, without hedging, I admit: I'm crazy about him!

I know from the first instant that it is not "serious," that I am one in a long, long list of women—before, after, and during. Raoul is not a man to confine his charms, or his bed, to one woman for more than the briefest of interludes. The episode lacks solidity, respectability, even monogamy in its own brief time; but I do not mean to sound unhappy or put-upon. I mean to sound lucky. Every woman needs one such man in her life—for champagne and caviar. In my time of famine, the Lord has provided! I can no longer remember, or even believe, that this much richness exists between a man and a woman. Only once before did I experience this heady excitement and pleasure; that man—simply by his memory—became the ghost lover in my marriage. His initials, by the wildest coincidence, were also R.B.; he now recedes to R.B. the First.

I meet Raoul through my work. The new project is not going well. I find it difficult to focus on my books and notes when so much attention and energy are diverted by events at home. A friend suggests I may get a fresh impetus from interviewing Dr. Browning—"I've heard him lecture, and he's dynamite!" I thank her for the suggestion, and reach Dr. Browning at his office. He's friendly, but sorry; he's leaving for Chicago that afternoon and will be gone for several days. The following week will be equally difficult for him. Unless, he adds as an afterthought, unless I want to meet him in the lobby of the Drake Hotel, have lunch, and cover what we can in a brief time.

A bird in the hand. I accept. Besides, it might be fun, and I am hard up for fun.

I type my list of questions for Dr. Browning with some apprehension. I am not yet sufficiently grounded in the field to interview an expert. Next week would be better. I put out two pens and a notebook. I dress quickly, but aware that I'm having lunch with a reputedly attractive man, I pick my new beige suit with a bright-orange scarf, and I spend an extra minute putting on blue eye shadow, even though I will, as usual, be a little late.

I walk toward the newsstand. That *has to* be Dr. Browning

—the lank tweed figure, the pipe, a narrow-brimmed hat, and leather patches at the elbows of his jacket. He deduces who I am at the same instant.

"Well, hello there!" He has a deep booming voice, full of laughter and the anticipation of pleasure. He tells me that he is surprised—and pleased—to find that the lady researcher has auburn hair, glowing color, and a good figure. He suggests a drink at the bar. At 11:30 A.M. liquor sounds almost sinful to me. I compromise with a sherry. Dr. Browning orders a double vodka martini. Since I am representing an august industrial firm on this project, I put up a small show of formality and dignity. I don't stand a chance. Dr. Browning is exuberant, full of his morning's good luck at locating an unusual mask for his collection. "You have a beautiful mouth," he says. Even a fifteen-year-old could recognize the signal. He is a downright seductive man, and as he turns the full force of his charm upon me, I am a willing victim.

"When were you divorced?" he asks me, without preamble. My eyes widen. I may even open my mouth in astonishment at his verbal parlor trick.

"You were obviously delighted to see me"—I am to learn, later, that Raoul never engages in simple questions and answers—"and I am more than delighted to meet you. We're going to be friends."

"How do you know?" I don't object, I'm simply curious. He laughs. He laughs a great deal in a beautiful basso that attracts glances from other tables. We are an obvious vignette: a man charming a woman, and the woman loving it! No shades are drawn.

He orders another double vodka martini for himself, and food for the both of us, which we do not eat. The notebook sits on the table with my pens. I do not get past the first question. I do not write a word. Dr. Browning talks about his work, the world of scholars in it, about his own views and opinions—never orthodox or sedate. Facts, names, wry comments, come spinning by me. I am fascinated. Any woman with her senses still intact would be intrigued with the man—the content, the wild attractiveness, and all now focused on me! If my head turns more quickly, more easily than other, more squarely anchored heads, I think: "That's *their* loss!"

"I'll be back from Chicago on Saturday, and I'll call you." He writes my telephone number on the back of an envelope and insists again that we are going to be great friends. I only half believe the cocktail-party conversation at twelve o'clock on a Wednesday. He must make his plane, and I must leave for an appointment across town. I blow out of the Drake with unexpected wind in my sails—a hazard in the heavy city traffic!

I hardly expect an encounter so overpowering, yet so ephemeral, to have a carry-over from Wednesday to Saturday. I also know Dr. Browning's reputation, so I do not sit and wait for him to call. Unexpectedly, he *does* call on Saturday, while I'm out, and leaves a message with Jill. "Who is Dr. Browning?" Jill wants to know, with her characteristically blunt curiosity.

"Oh—a man I've been doing some work with." And that becomes Dr. Browning's cover for the future.

He suggests we meet that evening, but I have plans. Alerted to the boy-girl game, I am pleased that I am truly *not* available on immediate demand. We make a date for Sunday. He has the afternoon in mind, but I explain that I play tennis on Sunday afternoons. He laughs a little and says he'll pick me up at six.

I plan to take a short rest after tennis, and a luxurious

bath. But I have an unexpected visitor, Lee McCay, a friend of many years who is deeply disturbed and in psychiatric treatment. Her face does not hide her angry sadness. I am making a fresh pot of coffee when she breaks down, sobbing. "All women over fifty should be done away with. No one would care." Strong, bitter stuff. I cannot make light of what her words must mean, but neither do I know how to handle it. Her tears are angry and demanding: "Love me!" "Help me" is the unspoken imperative. I am upset with her; with myself, but above all, at this minute I want her to go home. I want time to myself, to appear calm and at my best for the evening. Lee leaves me only ten minutes in which to bathe and dress. By the time Dr. Browning arrives, I am rushed and rattled. Not *so* rattled that I fail to notice Jill; she has planted herself in full view of the front door for a good look at this Dr. Browning as he walks in.

I am full of the difficult hour I have just spent and cannot keep myself from talking about it. But Raoul can listen as well as talk. He is an amazing man. He talks with stunning directness about women, men, relationships, and sex. Emotions are his raw materials. He is not afraid to think about them, and to express himself in Anglo-Saxon words. I find my mind leaping after him, lit by the wild rush of his talk. I have been self-encapsulated, dull, and insensate so long that I have almost forgotten the pleasure of exciting talk.

We go to a sober, genteel restaurant with black-brown paneling and diners as animated as the figures at a wax museum. It is hardly a sexy setting. But Raoul seems pleased. The waitresses make a huge fuss over him; he asks about their families, and their sore feet. They ask about his children. I sit quietly by in my simple black dress and pearls. I am detached, still—the amused observer. I'm from Missouri! I am not coy with myself. I have come to dinner with the intention of going back to his apartment if he asks me. We are both playing our parts in a patterned, understood game. But I am not throbbing to go.

I have his attention for the rest of the dinner. He has brought a gift for me, a charming foreign edition of Mother Goose rhymes. He has marked his favorites for me.

I warm up with the first martini.

"You don't have to lower your eyes for me," Raoul says. I did not realize I was doing it, shielding myself from his direct glance.

It is crazy. Impossible. Unbelievable. This man, who knows how to turn on a woman of any age, any size, or any shape, seduces me right at the table. My heart turns over, or maybe it is simply my glands, reactivated.

I poke at the food on my plate. I don't think I'm nervous about going back to his apartment, but it takes courage for me to be outspoken and to say, "I have some grim scars. . . . I don't want to be uncomfortable."

Raoul does not turn the subject away with polite avoidance. He asks what surgery I've had, how long ago.

A lamp is lighted, the radio is playing softly when we walk into his apartment. The game at the table was easier: all entangling words, anticipation, and the setting of a small fire. In spite of the one time with Cal, I am not practiced at getting into a strange bed. I want to pretend my scars do not exist. I want to be poised. I want to be great in bed!

I need not have worried. Raoul is running the evening. He kisses me, and it feels good, easy. He unzips the little black dress, and as I stand in my black bra and half-slip (carefully matched when I dressed), I experience a small, cool dread that mixes with the warm flush of my skin.

"Go into the bathroom and take some of this off."

I slide under the sheets next to Raoul—I know what I'm

doing. And part of me remains detached as I meet this man. I am in the hands of a professional. An expert. I think: "Every woman should try this." But soon it is no substitution or sublimation. Hank is not in the bed. Only Raoul and I are. It is an exciting, totally sensual night. A part of me, a very small part, stays observant still: "It's not so different, even with a man like this!" Then Raoul says, "You damned virgin!" Exactly what Cal said. I protest, but Raoul tells me not to fight it: "There's something appealing about innocence."

Afterward, propped up against the pillows, we talk—or Raoul does, about his work. He talks with the devotion of a scholar and the temperament of an artist, his mind lighted by his five senses. He is involved in color, line, light—as well as the sweat and motion of people going about their lives. He puffs on his pipe, grins, and talks with the pleasure of a collector about women he has known: young and beautiful, brainless and brilliant, thin and fat. "No—never fat. If you get fat, forget it!" he says.

It's over. Time to take me home. He is suddenly quiet. Walking down the hall to the elevator, I hold his hand for reassurance—like a small girl. I do not believe what comes next. Driving home along the deserted night streets, Raoul begins to discuss my research project; seriously, thoroughly, giving me the materials I went for Wednesday at the Drake. But he is wasting his time and talent. I am too filled with myself and the evening. I smile in the dark of the car—"*Vive la différence!*"

In my own house, I simply cannot go to bed. I play the piano, singing the Mozart as I play. If I never see Raoul again, I've had a taste of delicious excitement, been stirred, moved, and freed—the perfect antidote to the bitter dose of these last months. The trouble is that I want to see him again. "Don't be a fool! Act your age!" I caution myself. But I would like to be back in his bed the very next night, to sit up afterward in his bathrobe, talking, talking, talking.

He calls me often in the next months: from a hotel room in Cincinnati, in Denver; from his office; from his apartment at midnight. He will sometimes suggest that I "come over for a drink." On the very first of these spontaneous evenings, I see signs in the bathroom that another woman has been there recently. This is different from *knowing* about his reputation. Nevertheless, I walk into his bed with deliberation: a determination to get what I want out of the relationship.

My prescribed role doesn't last long. I am soon captivated. I do not allow myself to say I am in love with him, but I think about him with a secret excitement, hug the thought of him to myself, hold imaginary conversations with him. My mirror shows lights dancing in my eyes, my mouth turned up in a soft, secret smile. I am stirred to a new level of existence. Friends tell me "You look very well," with a note of surprise. I want to tell them "You'd look well, too, if . . ." I do not care that I risk discovery; that my actions could make my future even more uncertain.

Through it all, I recognize that I have been here before— in thrall to R.B. the First. Like Raoul, he was brilliant, charming, and erotic. Like Raoul, a seductive personality expressing himself as much in words as in the physical. Like Raoul, he knew about women; and knew that behind my poise and façade, I wanted to yield, wanted to be led. Each of these men, through his glance, his humor, his assessment of me, makes me the woman I want to be. Intoxicating stuff. No wonder I am not willing to be cautious!

I must do my share of waiting for telephone calls and invitations that do not come. I accept whatever conspiratorial intimacy Raoul offers—when he offers—and demand nothing. In part, it is my style with men; in part, my instinctive recognition that the slightest demand on my part will scare him away. I do learn to call *him*—to do it easily, flirtatiously.

We talk long hours on the telephone, talk long hours when we are together. He is usually "on"—ebullient, amusing. But there are times when he, too, scrapes bottom. I find him human enough, in the ways that a husband is human. He washes his own socks, has far too many patent medicines in his bathroom, drinks steadily, and, for so freewheeling a man, is painstakingly careful about every detail of his work, his car, and his health! I may be reading into his life out of a sensitivity to the aloneness of my own, but I sense a lack of structure, a quality of pathos. Raoul's wife left him. Obviously, too many women. And yet I see him as more emotionally than physically promiscuous! He even tells me "I like the courtship better than the realization." He talks wistfully about his children, and sardonically about Alice, his ex-wife—"She is intelligent, but not bright!" He tells me they tried marriage counseling before the separation, and I amuse myself thinking of this irrepressible man submitting to the cut-and-dried counsel of therapists I have known. Occasionally, he will talk to Alice on the telephone while I'm at the apartment. He makes a boy scout effort to sound friendly, polite, concerned about the children and their schooling. I comment only once after he hangs up: "You must have been a hard man to get over!" Raoul speaks with more commitment of a woman he was involved with who recently died. He is romantic, and true to her memory. I cannot help wondering: "Was he monogamous while she was alive?"

We *have* become friends, just as he predicted. Maybe it

is not all that I could wish for, but we do have a special relationship—and I have outlasted dozens of other women. The sexual attraction is the sparkle, the excitement for me, but it is far more than a sexual affair. I go to bed with him whenever he invites me, gladly; but I also treasure the long evenings when we talk, when he shares his vast knowledge. We exchange favorite books with each other, discuss what is happening in the news, talk open-endedly about the nature of men, women, and children. He gets into the habit of reading his manuscripts to me in their first-draft stage. He is a formidable scholar and at times the material is far beyond my reach. But he is also lucid, and a superb teacher; soon I become familiar enough with the major issues in his field to suggest changes, reorganizations, cuts in his papers.

Occasionally we play out small domestic scenes. I will stop by to heat canned soup for him when he is ill. Or I will carry over a casserole and serve dinner in his apartment. "I don't let every woman into my kitchen," he calls out to me from the living room. I smile down at the salad I'm mixing, and reply only to myself: "But you're not so discriminating about your bed!"

It is not a total idyll for me. What woman relishes taking her part in a procession of women? Knowing that the moment will pass, that it has neither roots nor responsibilities? Only once in our many evenings does Raoul see me down in the elevator and out to my car in the dark parking lot. For him, this may come under the heading of discretion, not bad manners. But I miss the caretaking aspects of marriage.

I do not always tamp down my reactions successfully. On one occasion, we must both attend the same meetings in Washington. We travel together, and I think surely he will suggest spending the night with me. That evening he comes up to the entertainment suite of the company that sent me, kisses me casually, has a drink, and leaves. I am all dressed up emotionally—with nowhere to go!

I turn back to the crowded, noisy room and pick out a large, nice-looking man with a twinkle in his eye and a drawling Western accent. He takes me to dinner. I doubt that we have ever read the same book, perhaps not even the same magazine. He talks about his daughter, about the wife who left him because of his "whiskey and women." I listen and suspect he is still "married" to his ex-wife.

"You and I have only one wife, one husband," I tell him, "the rest is play acting."

When we leave the restaurant, he tells the taxi driver to go to his hotel. I tell the taxi driver to go to mine.

"But I have a big bed," he says.

"What makes you think I'm going to bed with you?"

"You haven't been invited yet!"

I can tell just from the way he holds my hand that he's majored in women. We have a drink at *my* hotel, spar a little, and he walks me to my door. I cannot ask him to leave. I cannot turn virginal and chaste after leading him on all evening. Besides, I am angry and hurt because Raoul has not sent a message, obviously does not intend to come.

The sex with this stranger is businesslike. I am cold, thinking "What the hell am I doing here!" even while I know damned well he knows how to stimulate and excite a woman. Humorously, *he* cannot perform—he's had too much to drink; but he tells me, "You're small. If I'd been able to get it up, you'd be mighty sore in the morning." I am taken aback by such direct dealings. When he leaves, I try to slough off the experience. The next day when I catch sight of him at the meetings, I dodge—and blush. I do not want to meet him again.

I continue to live dangerously—so long as Raoul continues

to call me, to invite me. Once during the spring holidays when both Erika and Jill are away, I invite Raoul to the house. I refuse to concern myself with what the neighbors might think. We have an evening of lovemaking, talking, and food. But I do not feel carefree, as I do at his apartment. We are in the bedroom, the kitchen, the living room I've shared with Hank. My other life.

Why do I accept the limited part of himself that Raoul offers? Why am I uncritical of *his* shortcomings? Why do I let my guard down so successfully? Because he is brilliant and charming, because his eroticism arouses my own, or because he offers me a male leadership that permits me to take a passive role? On the other hand, it has none of the solid meat-and-potato protectiveness and concern that Hank offered me. Raoul should have been an affair within the marriage. A Roman candle, lighting up the solid marital ground!

Before the year is up, Raoul receives a new appointment at a university in the Southwest: more than two thousand miles away. Oddly, I am glad he is going. This can be a gracious exit line. He is strong medicine; so long as he continues to call, with his deep, seductive "Well, hello there!" I will half wait for, half expect the calls.

I do not know what will come next, but I am a bird freed from its cage of anger, pain, nonrelating. I still remember some of our conversations verbatim. Expressions he used still sound in my ear, and sometimes turn up in my open speech. On nights when I drive over the highway that leads to his former apartment, I remember my anticipation of pleasure.

CHAPTER XIII

Life Can Be Beautiful—or Can Life Be a Soap Opera?

A sense of precariousness is loose in the land.
—ANTHONY LEWIS, *The New York Times*

MEANWHILE, BACK in my *real* life, I am playing a part in my own soap opera, mastering my cues and my lines. There is always a happening: a disagreement or a difference pyramided to importance by the telephone calls and meetings, and by my propensity to be easily disquieted.

Hope by hope, the financial arrangement engineered with the help of Julia and John Borden falls apart. Hank thinks I should give the girls their spending and clothing money out of the check he sends me. That's not what we agreed upon, I protest, and look to Julia and John to back me up. They demur. They don't want to be put in the middle, not of this small, unpretty matter. Even Jill moves aside: "Don't involve me. Fight it out between yourselves." So once again, monetary matters are thrown back to the lawyers, and I am back on Alan's doorstep.

During this period I make conciliatory overtures to Hank.

"For the sake of the children, let's talk things out. Let's keep this from becoming ugly." Stale lines to fit a stale situation. I see Hank occasionally, and we confine ourselves to talk about money and the children. He never again mentions coming back for weekends, and I understand; in the atmosphere of dissension over money, this would be grotesque. Besides, from what I hear, I assume that Leslie is well established at the apartment. And I am seeing Raoul.

On a midweek evening, I meet Hank for a drink at a neighborhood restaurant. I arrive wearing Erika's camel's-hair school coat and my loafers, looking as though I might be going to the supermarket. I am my usual five minutes late. I was talking to Raoul until the last possible moment and did not leave myself time to dress. But I am buoyant, smiling. Nothing hurts. I suggest, almost as soon as I sit down with Hank, that we get down to the business of the evening: How to discard old wives. I am beyond suffering this evening. To be meeting with Hank, to go over the same old ground about money and legal arrangements, is not even relevant when I feel happy and radiant. I have lost Hank, but I've found something better. It does no good to remind myself that Raoul is temporary, that I do not exactly "have" him.

Hank half smiles, not certain whether I am bitter or unexpectantly flippant. Any *woman* could have guessed in an instant why I am so high-humored, but Hank doesn't have much time. He's due at a chess match. He's plainly relieved to find I'm not my earnest, seeking-truth-and-justice self tonight. We don't accomplish much; as he hurries off, I wonder, "What does 'Leslie baby' do alone in the evening? Fix her hair, her nails? Knit?"

Another evening, in another restaurant, the game is harder. My barometer of confidence and pride is lower. Raoul hasn't called in several days. Erika is alternately despondent and manic; she spends long hours staring at television—and the rest, irritating me. I am concerned. Hank looks withdrawn, slightly sullen. I know at first sight that I can get nothing from him, though God knows what I had come to get. Sympathy? A bit of problem sharing? A remnant of the old togetherness with which we'd raised Erika and Jill?

"I want a divorce," Hank announces. "Why won't you give me a divorce?"

I remember Lenore Coleman's advice: "Under no circumstance should you give Hank a divorce!" So I act shy, confused. "I'm not ready for a divorce." And my *next* lines could slip unnoticed into the daily segment of a soap opera. "I won't box you in. I know you cannot bear to be boxed in. If, in a year, you still want it, I will give you a divorce."

Hank agrees; and it is understood that he will do the same for me.

It is still only five months after separation; there is still the infinity of possibility open to each of us. I tell Hank that I must have the signed financial agreement so I can be free. "Free for what?" he asks. I repeat doggedly that I just want to be free. But Hank takes a tack of his own: "Too bad you won't go out and have some fun!"

I am angered by the implication that I have not found someone, as he has, that I will not "loosen up!" I want to brag: "If you only knew!" But caution is a stronger impulse. If I am fool enough to confide in him, he can use the information against me. He could even divorce me!

The crises keep coming with a wearying, repetitive quality. There's a limit to the number of times I can summon adrenalin, tears, anxiety, but I cannot allow myself to become bored. I must pace myself, like a runner preparing for my particular version of the Boston Marathon. And yet, even with tension, perplexity, and threat, separation must boil down to just one more tough, ongoing problem. What *was* my life for so long is resurfacing: work, children, friends come back into focus.

It is time. I am giving my first dinner party without Hank. I am still fastening my hostess skirt, dabbing Futur behind my ears when the first guests arrive. The casserole of chicken with green peppers and orange juice is in the oven, giving the house an aroma of "something delicious." The Borsault is out, to soften at room temperature. The port has been decanted. I have worked all day on the details but I have forgotten cigarettes and extra ice! These were always Hank's chores.

We are a small group, deliberately chosen; not our closest friends, but lively, bright people who will not make the evening too reminiscent. It is good to have the talk, warmth, color, good food in the house once more. I am too busy to be awkward as I sit in Hank's place at the head of the table. But in the half hour after the guests leave, I feel his presence by his absence. It is lonely now. No one to chat with as I empty ashtrays, collect liquor glasses, stack the dishes. No one to say "It was a good dinner" or "Go on up, I'll be along in a few minutes."

I do not look for a job, but one finds me: a three-day-a-week job tailored to my abilities. I consider it another "God will provide." Against Alan's advice, I take the job. "If your case ever comes to court, the judge will take into account that you are working; and you will not receive full support." Alan's considerations will have to be secondary. I need the fresh environment, the challenge—and the money. Again, I decide to live dangerously.

After the initial stage fright, I begin to enjoy the novelty of an office with sharp pencils, paper clips, a secretary to do my mail, and a boss to tell me what to do. I am a little scornful of coffee breaks and gossip, but I soon get into that swing. My work is well received, and the notes from my department head telling me I've done "a first-class professional job" are more rewarding than the checks and the raise. I am soon invited, even urged, to join the staff full time. The job helps me overcome some of my dependency fears: I *can* earn a living, whether or not I wish to live on it. Equally important, the job gives structure and focus to my day. The routines, the challenge of the work, help to organize the chaos within me.

But the job makes me the "man" of the house in a way my more independent work never did. At least once a month, I travel a thousand miles or more on assignment. The arrangements at home for the girls are makeshift, and I am not easy in my mind. Also, hotel rooms in strange cities— even de luxe rooms on the expense account—are lonely, not holiday fare.

On an everyday basis, I leave the house before eight and return through heavy evening traffic after six. I am often one very tired, grumpy parent. "Quit, if you're tired" is Jill's logical, if not sympathetic suggestion. My image as a mother is taking a drubbing at my own hands. I see myself as I think they must see me now, rushing about the kitchen in the morning to have my coffee, to empty the dishwasher, to run a load of laundry and transfer it to the dryer. No matter how early I get out of bed, I am always rushing, always surprised to find I'm going to be late for work again!

I come home carrying a bag of groceries in one arm, some reading from the office in the other; I must hurry to cook dinner. On far too many evenings, I want nothing more after dinner and the dishes (which *I* usually do to avoid starting a civil war) than to sit numbly in front of a television set and get to bed early with my music and that morning's *New York Times*. I am sodden in this scene, my sense of humor, my usual energies and interests drained away. I feel dull, martyred, and resentful. I do not like this role, but I cannot fight out from under it. I worry; I have known always that children gravitate to "where the life is." And life with Mother, at this juncture, is at low ebb!

I have delayed talking about Erika and Jill at any length because the story of how separation affected them, and influenced me as a mother, is complex and sensitive enough to be a book of its own. Separation does its damage here from the first moment.

With the extravagant anger of the young, Erika and Jill devalue all that has gone before. The family life that has nurtured them becomes a retroactive "lie," dishonored down to the last sentimental bits and pieces. "It was not real," Erika tells me with bitterness when I assure her there were many good things, many good times.

"How are the girls taking it?" I am often asked; but the same friends answer their own question: "Well—they're not young anymore." Clearly, they mean it is easier for me because Erika and Jill are past "child care," easier for the girls because they are old enough to "understand." Besides, I'm reminded, they'll soon be leaving home themselves.

True, Erika and Jill are eager and chafing for separation of their own. But they want to leave an intact home behind them: a museum for their memories, a storehouse for their leftovers, a base they can touch lightly, and leave again when they wish. They do not want a forcible dissolution of their "home."

A friend who is a therapist tells me that children will ac-

cept the parents' separation if their own lives are not too upset. Erika and Jill have school as usual, play hockey, stop for
Cokes at the local Howard Johnson, spend the same hours
on the telephone with their friends. Erika gets a Christmas
job at Gimbel's, where she charms the customers and con-
fuses the computer with her unusual arithmetic. Jill sings in
the school glee club and takes driving lessons. The same-
ness and structure in their lives is reassuring to the three
of us.

And yet the change *is* radical. Evenings and weekends
when we are together in the house, the atmosphere is thin
and unsatisfying. We are now three females, eating together,
watching television, coexisting—and we miss the leavening
quality of Hank's humor, his pipes, and his businesslike approach to problems. We miss him. When we tangle we need
him as our Solomon. More important than any visible detail
is the environment; willy-nilly, the girls are drawn into my
circle of uncertainty and antagonism.

Both girls are thoughtful conspirators, protecting me from
the knowledge of the woman Hank is living with. Even when
they know I know, Jill does no talking. Erika tells me: "If
it weren't so sad, it would be funny, Mom. She's a lot like
you!"

Like children—like people—Erika and Jill are often demanding, critical, seeing only their own interests. But they
are also sweetly protective and loyal toward me. Erika urges
me to cry, to let it out; she tells me I'm down in the dumps
because I'm home so much. Jill, less apt to deal with her
own or anyone else's feelings, tells me I behaved "like a
lady!" Jill, who could remind me reprimandingly in the early
months that "we're unhappy, too," finds me sobbing helplessly at another time and reassures me—in her way: "Don't
cry. I think you're a good mommy!" She puts her cool young

hand on my head. We change parts, and I am the child. She brings me tea and crackers, and orders me back to sleep.

Because we are thrown together so much, I fall into the habit of giving extra weight to what the girls say to me, to what they think. I assume that their perceptions are at an adult, rather than a teen-age, level. "They know," "Kids really understand," I say, in the offhand, slipshod way in which we credit the young with an intuitive wisdom. But I now think differently. At sixteen, they cannot have adult responses. They do not come trailing clouds of either pre-science or glory. They know and understand only what the limited canvas of their lives permits them to understand. What *is* pressingly present is not a supposed wisdom, but their own share of fear, disappointment, desire.

Erika and Jill are grown enough to comment and criticize, young enough to be ruthlessly, heedlessly outspoken. Their words often repeat in my head during the quiet before bed-time or in my first morning consciousness.

"Forget it, he's never coming back!" Erika tells me. She is concerned because I am "too easy," "too polite," because "I want to keep the door open." With the assurance of six-teen, Erika plans to marry Bart, the boy she's going with that moment, and explains to me: "We're not going to live like you and Daddy. We want to do everything together. You and Daddy didn't do things together." She stirs the memory of my intention to be better at marriage than *my* parents. I think sadly but lovingly, with hope, not sarcasm—"I hope you will!"

Jill assures me that she "understands" what happened. "Daddy explained that you were two totally different people."

Later, in the silence of my mind, I try to answer her, try to defend the marriage that brought her into being:

"Things are not always what they seem. Yes, it is true we were different; we thought differently, had different ideas about what to do with our lives, with our time. I played tennis, and Daddy played chess. I liked to travel; he liked to be at home. But we both breathed; we both had needs not easy to see or to categorize. We knit our existence together, flawed though it may have been, with habits, the furrowed places in the bed, children. It was our style, our lifetime. Yes, we *were* different, and might have gone on for twenty more years with the same admixture of affection and bitterness, loyalties and disappointments."

Erika, in her beguiling, headstrong way, is the more conspicuous problem, as always. When Hank was at home, he was an indulgent but anxious father, and Erika and I often allied ourselves against his seemingly needless concern. She and I would signal each other that "Daddy's making a fuss again!" But with Hank no longer playing the "heavy," I inherit the role. I become strict and anxious—somebody has to be! Erika and I fight toe to toe on matters of school attendance, hours, her responsibilities in the house. With Hank gone, she senses my depleted power; and she moves in. One night during her little-theater experience, she is later than usual. I watch the clock at two, at two-thirty, at three-thirty—and she is still out. Where do I turn in the middle of the night? I call the police. A meaningless gesture. They have no record of any accident or incident involving a tall, beautiful girl of sixteen. They suggest that I call the hospitals.

I call Hank. "Erika is not home yet."

"What can *I* do?" is his response. And I am left alone and afraid until she shows up, arrogantly disclaiming any need for my being upset. "I didn't ask you to wait up for me. It's your problem!"

Another day. She wants the car, but I need it. I am explanatory: I am working full time; I have a tight schedule. In the quick call-up of conflict, her violet-blue eyes get fighting cold and she tells me: "Think of somebody besides yourself." . . . "It's the principle," she argues. "You ought to loosen up!" I am slapped by her words. I walk out, slamming the door. My anger redounds to Hank. I feed it. He left me alone to handle this. He can afford to be generous and good-natured, while I must become the disciplinarian, fighting off the flak of everyday living.

I *know* that Erika will stop in at Hank's office the next day—barefoot, her dark, gleaming hair long and loose, knowingly ingenuous—to enlist his sympathy. Erika has always known how to get between us, to play one against the other, to get her own way—when we allowed it. Ben advises me: "If Hank wants to cater to her, don't interfere. Let her be. Let her work it out with him. Throw her a life preserver if she turns to you."

Jill is another matter. Another worry. She has eyes the color of sherry held up to the light, chestnut hair cut in a cap to her face—a pretty face; all the components of a lovely young girl, except the ability to soar, to be easy and free with herself or anyone else. She is fighting fiercely against Erika's wont to fill the house; against me, because she says I am "managing" her life. I have no alternative but to shrug and worry. Yet unbeknownst to me, she is somehow learning to be charming, conversational—with others. I hear her practicing on the telephone with Hank. Sometimes, in her effort to be "interesting," she will tell him what I'd rather he did not know. But I understand; she does not want to "lose" her father emotionally or financially. I respect her need, and am encouraged that she is making her own relationship with him.

148

Even as I write that last sentence, I shake my head. I am not being totally honest. I *do* and I *don't* want the girls to make their own relationship with Hank. A great deal of pious talk centers around "the children" in separation and divorce; surface words, not true even as they are being mouthed. Under this acceptable blanket of concern is hidden the struggle to attract the sympathy, the affection of the children, to "win" in the separation conflict.

I want all of my daughters' sympathy, all of their loyalty. I want them to know that I am hurt, vulnerable, and alone; that Hank is not giving me enough money; that I am worried about my future, physically as well as economically. I want to be their "better" parent. And I want them, possessively, to be *my* children. No one's attitude, no one's loyalty matters more to me than that of Erika and Jill. But Hank has an advantage; he's the "sunshine" parent, treating them to a good dinner in a restaurant, offering a sympathy and detachment that is harder to come by in the day-to-day frictions under the same roof. I see myself as short of good humor, money, and energy; long on discipline and disagreeableness. I think bitterly: "Hank can afford to be good-natured and fun—once a week; and children go, inevitably, where it is livelier, more cheerful."

It is hard for me to admit, but Hank and I, without ever putting it into words, are in competition for our own children.

Alan Springer warned me at the start: "In fighting for yourself, you may alienate your children." He was referring to money matters. The idea, when he first put it out, was atrocious, impossible. It does not happen exactly as he forewarns, but I *do* find myself, consciously separating my interests from that of the girls—for the first time. "They're young," I rationalize, "with all their lives ahead of them, while I am vulnerable to physical threat, to financial insecurity." By good fortune, it never comes to a drastic choice. But living with the knowledge that my interests can be separate—even competitive—with my children's is a humiliating, unenjoyable discovery. One of the uglier lessons of separation.

Before we have a signed agreement, I cannot be sure that Hank will voluntarily pay the forthcoming college bills. I confide my fears to Erika, who, because of extra credits, is searching for a college a year earlier than Jill. She is shaken. But she comes back from the next dinner with Hank and reports elatedly: "Daddy's going to pay for college—anywhere I want to go. He says there's plenty of money!"

"Well—I was afraid for nothing."

"Yes," she chides me, "why did you have to worry me?"

Why, indeed? Because I was frantic and alone, and, in my unwisdom, had overestimated Erika's maturity. I had attempted to share my anxiety. I had momentarily forgotten the cannibalistic element of children toward parents: get what you need—cajole, scream, argue, but get it!

In an effort to smooth over my error, I compound it. Why not visit the colleges with Hank, I suggest to Erika; make him feel part of it? I sound to myself like a self-conscious, manipulative human-relations specialist out in industry. Erika catches it: "Why do we have to play games?" She is so real; and my realities, by contrast, sound cheap. Hank has become the enemy, and I am thinking with the cunning of a fox at bay. Not a picture of myself I like—or would willingly reveal to my daughter.

There is one critical episode I am loath to relate—it can still make me cringe. But if I hold back, my point would be lost: that I now do what I never suspected I could do. This involves "getting the evidence" that Hank is living with another woman. Even the phrase is stagy, hyperdramatic for us.

The idea is first suggested to me by most ethical, principled friends: "You may not like it" is their prelude, and their conclusion is "You have to do what is necessary." No one comes out and says "Hire a private detective." Alan Springer agrees to it, if *I* will find the detective and make the arrangements. I am embarrassed even to make inquiries. But a friend who has been through a dramatic and traumatic divorce gives me the name of a local detective.

Even in our brief telephone conversation, I find the man a boor. But I have taken the step. He tells me he cannot get past the doorman in Hank's apartment house, that he has no way of entering. Can *I* arrange to have him let in?

It's certainly not like the movies. I did not bargain for anything this involving. But I learn that Hank is going on a holiday with Leslie that weekend and that Erika will have the apartment key in order to feed the cat.

We are two deceitful, criminal-like children, arranging to let the detective in. Erika opens the door to him, and the man rummages through the apartment until he finds Leslie's personal mail and belongings. He reports triumphantly to me that it is a "haul" of evidence.

But I am more concerned because I *let* Erika become involved, contrary to every canon of child raising and decency. It is an episode I cannot expunge from my conscience.

Yet if I were to be hardheaded about it, these photostats, presented as incontrovertible evidence that a woman is residing in Hank's apartment, will have great bearing on everything that happens thereafter. For we do, in spite of any odds I would have given, we *do* have our day in court.

CHAPTER XIV

A Day in Court

Try to remember when life was so tender . . .
—THE FANTASTICKS

I DO NOT believe it will happen. But it does. Hank and I go into court about money.

On a fresh green May morning Alan drives me to the county courthouse. The beauty of the countryside makes the business of the day even more shoddy and implausible, clearly at loggerheads with my "prewar" perspective. Beneath my apparent poise and a seeming interest in what Alan is saying to me—that I must accept what happens in court with good grace, whether or not it is decided in my favor—I pretest my capacity to go through the day. As Alan and I drive the thirty minutes to court, I must work to keep control. I wonder if he knows.

I do not want to act badly, to make a fool of myself. This is to be the day in court for the irrational picture of myself: for the put-upon, discarded wife; for the virtuous woman who has had unjust desserts for her years of devotion. I am disembodied, and expect that like a delayed time bomb, I will do my reacting afterward.

Alan guides me through a labyrinth of drab, narrow basement corridors to Room A, where our hearing will be held at ten o'clock. Brian Carrigan, our county lawyer, is waiting. Three strong, we walk into the sparsely furnished, dark basement room that is masquerading as a courtroom. Hank is already seated on one side of a scarred wooden table, flanked by David Elkan, his "intown" lawyer, and his county lawyer, a vulnerably young man with pink cheeks, wearing an ill-fitting navy-blue suit. I never do catch his name.

The lawyers greet one another affably, in the manner of men who know that in the next case they may be on the *same* side.

I look directly at Hank. Everything about him is familiar, warm, and, in some vestigial way, mine. I am closer to him than to anyone in the room. Does he see the absurdity of so many strangers come together to argue about *our* lives, to take part in our personal theater of the absurd? The dreary basement room, with its high, small windows, is a Pinter setting, and Hank and I are acting out the ineffable sadness of two lives that tried to join, that did join and touch, without achieving their vision of touching each other at the living center. I see it in a glaring light; it is not "who is weak" or "who is strong," "who gave more," "who loved more." But each of us, hurt in our beginnings, so little practiced in closeness, could not by the magic act of marriage achieve what our lives did not prepare us for.

Absurd or no, the legal comedy has its own precise ceremonies. "Hear ye, hear ye, the court is in session"—just as we see it done in movies, on television. We all rise as the judge enters, looking, in spite of his black robes, far more like an insurance salesman than a pensive, judicative figure. The four lawyers approach the bench to discuss procedures with the judge.

While their backs are turned, I look at Hank again. I smile. I don't know whether it's my manners or my autonomic nervous system. Am I too friendly? I cannot help myself. Surely Hank is the only other one in the room who sees the comedy. I say in a quiet, conspiratorial voice, "If you don't write about this, I will!"

Hank can't quite make me out, but he acknowledges my friendliness with a slight shrug. I realize he is tense, concerned with what is to come.

Brian Carrigan, my county lawyer, has come alive from the pages of John O'Hara. Six feet tall, with a handsome bearing, and florid good looks untroubled by undue introspection. He hunts—I'll bet. And his diet must consist of steak and prosperity, strong liquor and weak-willed women. The instant the case gets under way, Brian becomes the dominant figure in the room. He is shrewd, quick, and self-assured; he *knows*, as he rocks back slightly onto the heels of his heavy cordovan shoes, that he is authoritative, competent, and important in his small pond. He talks to the judge as though he were planning to play a round of golf with him the next Wednesday afternoon. The two men undoubtedly serve on the same governing boards in the community. They are equals.

The dice are loaded on our side. Next to Brian Carrigan's assurance, Hank's county lawyer is a bumpkin, raw with his youngness, deferential to the bench.

We have waited to appear before this particular judge because he is in favor of God, country, and mothers. Brian is planning to show Hank as a man who left a faithful wife and who is now living openly in luxury with another woman. It is the luxury, *not* the other woman, that is calculated to cut the mustard. The judge, who lives a carefully circumscribed life on a fixed income, will, predictably, take a jaundiced view of a husband who enjoys the benefits of an expense-account economy—a car, membership in clubs, credit cards—and yet is niggardly about what he gives his wife and children.

Brian rapidly presents his case: a husband who is not providing sufficient support. The nub of the matter is how much Hank really does earn.

Hank is sworn in and answers Brian's questions.

> Is his car an office expense?
> Yes.
>
> Does he use it personally?
> Well, sometimes.
>
> Does he use credit cards for gasoline?
> Sometimes.
>
> Does he invite guests, including his daughters, his father, the Bordens, to the club when the bill is paid for by the office?
> On occasion.
>
> Does he have his haircuts at the club, as an office expense?
> Well—yes.
>
> Is he now residing at the given address with a woman named Leslie Maron?

Hank refuses to answer this last question on the grounds that it will incriminate him. Until that moment, I did not realize that his affirmative would be tantamount to admitting adultery, which is a legal offense in the state.

Brian submits in evidence the photostatic copies of Leslie's bank account, letters addressed to her at the apartment, and store bills sent to Hank's address—all procured by the detective. I am uncomfortable. Doesn't Hank wonder how Carrigan obtained these?

Hank is taking a legal licking. But he handles himself well. He is as straightforward as he can safely allow himself to be, well spoken, and more at ease than I would have imagined. But I find him surprisingly naïve in this situation, and not well counseled. Yet he is appealing that morning. I like him. I even feel warm enough to think it might be love. What would Ben Diamond make of that?

It is now my turn. Both Alan and Brian have instructed me to say as little as possible, and to look helpless. Alan also suggested beforehand that I make an effort to look expensively dressed. This is not my style. I doubt that any man in that courtroom, except Hank, appreciates the understatement of my hundred-dollar white cotton dress, the low-heeled pumps, and the pearls, which were an anniversary gift from Hank. I sit in the chair close to the judge's bench and I am no one I know. I could be the dummy to Brian Carrigan's ventriloquist as I answer in a low, careful voice cleared of emphasis or feeling. My voice does not waver or crack; I even find myself getting into the swing, taking on the persona of the poor wife who has been left after a severe illness, who faces more surgery in the future.

Hank's lawyer now questions me about my expenditures for food, clothing, and the upkeep of the house. When I say that I spent more than a thousand dollars for clothes in the past year, Hank looks astonished, turns to David Elkan and whispers. David then asks if I have the canceled checks. I do. Hank shakes his head again, in denial, convinced that I am lying. "You didn't," he says later; he is unwilling to believe that I would either lie *or* spend a thousand dollars! He still has high standards for me. He simply does not recognize that each step taken in this courtroom is ritual, a standard performance predicated on the "morals" of adversary marital law.

I find the court procedure far too swift to be accurate. Bald statements become incorrect through incompleteness, through failure of the lawyer on either side to explore or challenge. No one asks me, for example, if I am or have been working. The courtroom scenes are done far better on television.

At noon we adjourn for a luncheon recess. Alan joins Hank and David Elkan to see if something can be settled "out of court" before readjournment. Brian Carrigan invites me to lunch at his country club. He is driving a powder-blue Cadillac convertible. Over drinks, I flirt with him, but he does not respond. I am only mildly rebuffed. "I'm not his dish of tea," I tell myself. "What could he possibly want with a woman who thinks too much?" During lunch, Brian refers to Hank as "that poor bastard."

When we return to courtroom A, Alan informs me that I must make a swift decision. Hank and his lawyer are now willing to make an out-of-court settlement. Do I want to accept it, or see the court proceedings through to a finish that afternoon? Alan adds: "Hank says he does not need a divorce at this minute." I know why. I have been told by Julia that "Leslie baby" is gone. Hank discovered that she was an alcoholic!

I must make my decision in the minutes before the judge returns from lunch. I am carried along by the excitement, the drama, the anything-can-happen quality of a day in court. But I am, in truth, also weary of the prolonged negotiations. I do not trust the lawyers to act any more swiftly now than they have in the past. It will be a relief to let a third party make an arbitrary decision. I decide to gamble: let the court hearing run its course.

The judge's award is a bombshell. Two hundred dollars *more* a month than I had expected. More than I asked Hank for originally. However, the judge adds, his verdict is temporary; we must come back into court after a few months with more detailed financial information. No doubt, Brian Carrigan rocking back on his expensive, well-heeled shoes has carried the day. Without knowing or caring who Hank and I are, what the true circumstances were, he has played his part to perfection.

I am elated. I have won. It is like winning at roulette—a glorious giveaway, an end to my money troubles. Yet I am uneasy. It's not fair. I do not want to do this to Hank, to take more than I'm entitled to. I know there will have to be consequences. There are always consequences.

Alan is jubilant about the judge's decision—and surprised. "Now we have leverage for bargaining," he explains. But I am thinking more about Hank's astonishment, his hurt as he leaves the courtroom. I didn't want to do that to him. He's already had one blow, the breakup with Leslie. He'll feel that everything is going against him. I am now uneasy, no longer elated. I am empathizing with Hank. It's a throwback to old habits.

Winning in court does give me leverage, but not Alan's leverage. I can approach Hank in a new way. I have something to offer: compromise, generosity, fairness.

Part Four

Reinvolvement

CHAPTER XV

Re-enter Hank

You may not litigate by day, then copulate by
night . . .

　　　　　—JUDGE, DENYING A PETITION FOR
　　　　　DIVORCE

H O W D O E S it happen that almost a year to the day that
Hank walked out—a year of another woman for him, other
men for me, of legal sparring that culminates in our day in
court—how does it happen that I am standing in Hank's
apartment, admiring the view from his balcony, masking
only lightly my curiosity about the furnishings, the magnificent hi-fi set, the outsize bed, and that, not unexpectedly, I
soon find myself *in* that bed?

We come together because I call Hank, tell him I want to
talk about money and the court verdict. I am still a mixture
of triumph and guilt, but I am able to call because Leslie has
moved out, because I have something to offer.

Hank agrees to see me. Remembering the Sunday morning
in the breakfast room when I was all yellow, orange, and
suppliant, I do not want him to come to the house. We
agree to drive out into the country.

As we start our evening, Hank is stiff and resistant, not at his most likable. But he cannot make me uncomfortable or defensive, no matter what his attitude. I am Lady Bountiful, offering.

I propose to Hank that "since the court has awarded me more than I asked for, why don't we take the amount you've been sending and the amount the court ordered and split the difference?" This is still my effort to write an agreement. Hank says he'll think about it, and the money matters are over. We stop at an inn for a drink, and I can feel Hank warming a bit.

With a seeming reluctance—but without forgetting that we tell others what we *want* them to know—I let Hank urge out of me the fact that there *have* been other men since he left. He swears on the heads of our children that he will not use the information against me—ever! Without names or details, I give him a synopsis of Cal, Raoul, and the one-night stand in Washington.

"You *didn't*— Did you *really?*" This is not his "reading" of me. He believes, as he told me at one of our meetings, that I cannot enjoy myself. Suddenly, I cease to be one of those excellent women who will never tempt a man to seduce her!

Now that I have confided this much to Hank, I am flustered. I do not want to give away "classified" information about myself; nor do I want to "tell" on any of the men. It would be disloyal *and* unwise. I am caught in my own provocative act. I am blushing and enjoying myself; being open, yet closed; wanton, yet chaste.

As a bargaining point, to encourage me to reveal more, Hank says, "I'll tell you whatever *you* want to know."

He never understands, now or later, that I do not want to

know all about Leslie, or any other woman. I know what is essential: that she has been, and that she is now gone. He tells me anyhow: "I've been freer than I've ever been. Anything goes—my way." I can see so many things that were at work in him: the need to free himself, to break old patterns; then there is the American husband's dream of the compliant Japanese-style wife who will symbolically bow and rub his back. It is all inseparable from the middle-aged male syndrome: the prodding worry that time is passing, that some better life has eluded him. I see this as a companion to Hank's wanting, years back, to leave his business and teach in Arizona, his wanting to go to Europe for a year, his need for something new, some novelty of life to relieve the dull stretches, his periods of apathy. What never emerges is any sense of who or what Leslie was, other than an ersatz Japanese wife.

In my mood of the moment, I say impulsively, "One night *we* ought to go to a motel."

"Would you like to?" He responds with a nice crinkly smile.

There is a new tone. Our relationship has come almost full circle to the teasing, exploratory beginnings of our first double date with Julia and John. I say good night as the motel "proposition" hangs lightly in the air. He can call me if he wishes.

Inside of a week Hank calls and suggests we meet in town for a drink. I drive in, smiling to myself, delighted, my anticipation adding more to my looks than all the attention I've given my dress and my make-up.

We go to a hotel bar, the kind of place to which we rarely went when we were "married." We drink, talk, laugh about unimportant things in the way that the dark rendezvous setting of a bar encourages. Hank says, without hiding his surprise, "You're more fun to take out than to be married to!"

I deflect the barb with some general comment on marriage. I'm not fool enough to pick up that hostile gauntlet!

Later, when we walk into his apartment, he half apologizes for the sparse look. "You'll have to imagine it full of furniture." Leslie's furniture, I presume. I am far more interested in the reality of what Hank was doing, where he was living, and how, during the period when I was tormenting myself, when my mind was feeding on its own pictures.

Here it is: the couch, throw rugs, air conditioner, dishes, spices, liquor in the cabinet. A white-and-orange color scheme. Delicate goblets of stark, modern design. These are the backdrop of his reality.

We talk about the surgery that has been prescribed, that I cannot force myself to schedule, in spite of the Damocles threat. In this area Hank is, as always, most sympathetic. It is a bridge from which we can move on. And we do. Into the bedroom.

It is truly exciting, physically thrilling, to have my own husband—a twenty-year husband—undress me. Find buttons on a dress he's never seen before. Straps. The bed is huge, and I roll around like a child, and giggle. And then he holds me. I am physical, and filled with feelings I could not sort out if I would. I am home in his arms, pleasured and hurt all at once. I hold back, wanting to be cool, not appearing eager, not pressing him with my wishes. But I nestle closer and closer. I kiss him back. Everywhere. And we have each other, simply, with great passion and warmth. No words. Nothing else is between us that night. In the bed, as often in the past, we are together, at ease with each other, yet fresh and novel. A rare moment in our lives. Doing only what each of us wants to do, what we could not stop ourselves from doing.

In the strange months that follow, I always know how friendly and warm Hank is feeling toward me by the amount of his solicitude. That evening he sees me to my car, insists that I lock the doors and drive carefully. I drive off smiling happily to myself. It has come so easily to be womanly and seductive with Hank. His willingness enables me to be so.

The next morning Julia calls. "Hank says you're still the most attractive woman around, the best company to be with."

In the second year of separation, I begin the adventure of seeing my own husband, who is not my husband. He calls me. Or I call him. If nothing else, I have learned in the year how to call a man. In the beginning Hank says "We ought to talk." He means about money and the still nonexistent financial agreement.

We never *do* talk about money matters. Not if I can help it. The subject can only turn us into natural adversaries, so I ruffle my girlish feathers, look helpless and confused. Hank is gallant, in a wry, amused way; it is accepted that talking about money upsets me, although he always adds "You've got to talk about it sometime."

On those first evenings, I arrive a little breathless, a little late, adding the scent of suburban air, French perfume, and freshly cleaned kid gloves to the haze of Hank's pipe tobacco. He accepts my hello kiss with a half smile which I interpret for myself: he is half glad to see me, half wondering what the hell we're doing here. I may be the curiosity-shop element in his life.

He asks what music I'd like to hear while he pours the

drinks. He's proud of his new record collection. I may have learned to call a man—he has learned to enjoy Brahms! We talk, more than we talked together for many years before separation. We are simply a man and a woman at our private cocktail party, taking each other's measure, exchanging signals on a sexual level; the words are about music, about the jet planes going past his window wall, about books, politics, or people.

At core, I am heady with the pleasure of being invited back. If I sense Hank's antagonism surfacing, if we knock against furniture of the past, I simply laugh and say "Don't be a hostile bastard," and curl around him on the couch, letting my shoes drop to the floor. Before long, we move to his outsized bed. Sometimes we find a restaurant open afterward. Sometimes we miss dinner altogether.

Nobody can naysay our right to be with each other, and yet there is a delightful, illicit quality. We do not exactly hide, but neither do we go out of our way to meet people we know. We have no precedent, no ground rules for *this* relationship. Perhaps no expectations. These early evenings are the freest we have known; for me, a carefree lark. There's an ease between us I'm hard put to remember in the marriage, and a piquant mixture of discovery and familiarity. There's an almost sexual charge in sharing the intimacy of Hank's bathroom, of finding my way in his kitchen.

All of this does not just happen. I have my small seductive ways. I can make advances, even physical advances; admit that I like physical attention, enjoy sexual excitement. It is not the pleasure but my capacity to speak of the pleasure that is new, that adds spice.

One night in bed Hank laughs aloud. I want to know what's funny and he says, "I'm thinking of sending my compliments to the chef!"

Hank is fascinated by the before and after of what he looks upon as my sexual reformation. I have not been consistent with his image of me. If I *know* that I have always been a passionate, sensuous woman—whether expressed or unexpressed—that I have learned most of what I know from him, not others, I do not insist upon it. I have learned finally what every woman may not know, but should know: not *how* to be dishonest, but simply *when* to be honest!

I take special satisfaction in attracting Hank again. Part of it is a small game I play. As often as I gracefully can, I say, "We're not married"; and each time, Hank replies, "But yes we are!" I get a small, perverse thrill out of making him say it, out of hearing it over and over. Perhaps I am proving I can have him—other men notwithstanding. But I think that on this basis alone, it must soon pall. The memories grow less and less important; it is not the memory of being held that warms me, but being held *now*.

And yet each time I know nothing is foregone, nothing predestined about a next meeting. Hank is gentlemanly, admiring, teasing. Always an ardent lover. Beyond that, he is totally uncommitted. He might as easily stop calling. He stays with the attitudes he took on at the time he left, protecting his contention that he was right to do as he did, and that he has done nothing since to be ashamed of. If I should press him ever so slightly, pull out one small resentment, one small martyrdom, I would bring forth a flood of defensive attitudes—and he would most certainly stop calling. On an evening that is not going too well—and we do have them —he will tell me I am "impossible" or that I'm a "wonderful woman—but I can't live with you." I sit back with my heady portion of vodka on the rocks and smile, without words.

In just such a setting one evening, Hank informs me that he is keeping all his options open. They include, as he lists them, the possibility of living alone, of finding someone new, of returning to me, and, surprisingly, of returning to Leslie! He has an occasional attack of conscience and declares when we are together: "I shouldn't be doing this!" I assume he is serving notice that his intentions are lightweight. I have a self-protective reply: "I'm here because I'm getting as much as I'm giving." A bit of bravado, a bit of the old soap opera, and my *bella figura*. Yet, all with a measure of truth. In that moment, I *am* content to be wanted in any way Hank evidences. I am not truly sure what more I want from him. I am not even sure—although I can hardly confide this to Hank—that his option to return to me *is* still open.

In the midst of our quasi affair, I cannot forget the salient fact that we still do not have a signed financial agreement. In a crazily contradictory way, I am playing two parts: smiling and engaging Hank of an evening; and the next day consulting with Alan about the latest details in the legal negotiations. I cannot be certain how long the present noncombative relationship with Hank will last. I am alerted, if not threatened, by his occasional remarks—"You're getting all my money" or "I can't afford *your* standard of living." No matter how lightly he puts these out, I am reminded afresh that I need the long-term protection of an agreement.

The lawyers, at this point, are still calling each other, still promising to "get back" to each of us with another minute development. The ending is still not in sight. I suggest, and Hank agrees, that we should cut through the waste motions. The four of us should sit down and talk it out. I "borrow" the idea directly from the movie about divorce that I mentioned earlier.

It is a strange meeting. I keep as quiet as possible and concentrate on looking incapable of understanding or managing my own financial future. Alan speaks for me. Only a few nights before, I was with Hank at his apartment. Now we are sitting across from each other, acknowledging each other politely. The three men discuss not only the separation agreement, but talk of an "understanding" that will be effective in case of divorce. Purely verbal, in view of the legal restrictions. Hank is at his most charming and good-humored, half jesting through the afternoon. "What happens if I meet a lovely girl on my way to the washroom, and we want to get married?" It is understood that I am to leave any money I may have to Erika and Jill, while he is then free to leave *his* money to the hypothetical second wife.

It's all a game. All playing. No blood. No antagonism. I am not above enjoying the element of intrigue, the small conspiracy between Hank and myself. Besides, the agreement seems to be coming into being, finally! We agree to agree, and as we finish the meeting, Hank says, "I'll buy you a sandwich." We leave together.

Neither lawyer expresses the slightest surprise or suspicion, but I wonder what they make of the sweetness and light. They are bright men, less corroded than most lawyers with legal jargon, regulations, and procedures. Yet I doubt, to this day, that they realize that our extralegal activities cooled the conflict, made us delightfully tractable, conciliatory clients.

In short, they did not make the agreement. We did.

CHAPTER XVI

The Revolving Door

The individual is the seat of a constant process
of decantation; decantation from the vessel containing the fluid of the future time, sluggish, pale
and monochrome, to the vessel containing the
fluid of the past time, agitated, and multicolored
by the phenomena of its hours.
                                     —SAMUEL BECKETT

A FEW months later, when the agreement is signed, it does
not become the rock, the shelter I envisioned. The "new"
relationship with Hank has shifts, changes, unevennesses. On
one evening, Hank and I will be close and content; another,
the space between us sodden and cool, the viability, the
vitality, gone. The uncertainty that centered so long around
the agreement is transferred to the question: What will
happen to Hank and me? Our time together has no shape,
no definitive pattern. I don't know where it is heading. As
always, I am eager for resolution, an ending. What I do not
realize is that I am now in a new segment of the soap opera,
and will be going through the revolving door for a long
while.

On a dozen different late nights as I drive home from Hank's apartment (worrying, as usual, about the possibility of a flat tire in the dark, empty streets), I tell myself: "It's over! We're through." Or more accurately: "It's over. *He's* through!" But Hank calls again—and I go. "He's more chronic with you than your ulcers," says Ben Diamond. His criticism is explicit: I cannot make up my mind to break off with Hank.

Ben is right. I follow Hank's lead, his wishes; I go along, reacting to each evening as it occurs, telling myself I am simply doing as I please.

The whole thing damned near falls apart when I go to Europe for two weeks. On the first Saturday I'm back, Hank and I have dinner. The restaurant is one of our favorites. I am glad to be there, and the evening, on the surface, is no different from other evenings. Yet I find myself talking too much. Hank is too quiet. All my conversation assumes a mutuality that is not quite there. I must be overreading, I tell myself; I am too quick to imagine.

Early the next week I receive a letter from Hank. Only one line. "I have taken up one of my options." Nothing more. Leslie has staged her comeback. I am not as stunned as I might be. Erika has already mentioned seeing Leslie around town with Hank.

I do not understand Hank. Isn't he foolish? If the girl *is* an alcoholic, the situation is self-defeating. I cannot even feel properly competitive toward a woman beset with more problems than I have. But I miss the telephone calls, the evenings together, being involved with a "steady" man. If I miss Hank himself, I do not dwell on it. In my effort to accept what I cannot change, I try to handle my feelings, to train them to command, like some pet poodle.

Besides, the episode is soon over. Leslie is gone—as I

speedily learn from the Bordens. I have little use for traditional pride. I hardly allow Hank a decent interval for mourning before I find a pretext for calling him, making it possible for *him* to call *me:* for dinner and the evening.

"My friend is gone," Hank announces a bit sheepishly when I arrive to find the spare contemporary apartment of which he is so proud now crowded with quattrocento chests, Third Avenue lamps and tables. I keep my instant reaction to myself: "You never let *me* move this kind of stuff in!" Meanwhile, Hank is still explaining. "All this is going. For good, this time."

If I am the concubine restored to favor at the expense of the one displaced, I do not dwell on the justice or injustice, dignity or indignity of my position. As a woman alone, I no longer know what I will do until the circumstances present themselves. For much of my life, I have ridden the high horse of principle. Principle, as I now see it, kept me from the scrabbling and sweating of ordinary mortals, but it also removed me from the heat, the occasional laughter, the unending exchange of humanity at a less lofty level. I am learning to be flexible, and it remains to be seen how docilely the principles will step aside.

Once more Hank and I pick up our strange, tenuous relationship. I cannot bring it into focus. Does it exist only because of sheer tenacity on my part, the same tenacity with which I got Hank originally? Or are we being held together by something important, an inevitability I cannot define? It often *looks* like any casual affair, with little or no reference to the years that went before; an affair that must wind down to an ending. But I know we are significantly more. We are the not uncommon phenomenon of the husband and wife, separated or divorced, who nevertheless gravitate toward each other. We are a minute repeat in an over-all pattern.

The divorce literature is filled with cases of men and women compulsively driven to see, talk, and sleep with each other—even if it jeopardizes the final decree. There are reasons. The fascination of trying to go home again, the challenge of rewriting a relationship, the inability to accept failure—and reasons that go beyond mere reasons.

It's almost a year now, and Hank and I no longer have the freshness of our new affair. We no longer treat each other with gloves-on courtesy. We have continuity and habit, and I find the old reasserting itself: old moods, old modes. Hank's peevishness when I speak too forthrightly; a dulled response to my enthusiasm; annoyance at criticism, if only implied. Yet he presses me to be open, in accordance with his psychological credo, and chides me because I am not honest. Of course I'm not! I hold back, not confident enough with Hank, not willing to reveal that I am not as cocky and self-contained as I seem; certainly not that there are some nights I am glad to be going home alone!

Hank still uses the word "aggressive" against me, and forces me to defend my words, my thoughts, my moves. As we replay these old tapes from the marriage, Hank skirts the question: Which of us erred? It is lightly assumed that it was I—but that I am now reformed, which makes it possible for Hank to see me, to be with me again. It is part of the game, the natural corollary to the many moves I've made toward Hank. Through the game, I catch a glimmer, now and then, of his old view of me as "wonderful."

When Hank emphasizes my sexuality, I don't think it's real, but it flatters me and tickles him to see his once-conservative wife in an almost libertine light. The sex, inevitably, grows less novel, no longer so fresh and piquant, but each of us is proving something. Hank is making a stand for his masculine prowess and skill, while I am determined to prove my femininity, my capacity to yield. Exactly those things once on trial in the marriage bed. Yet our physical intimacy can often be sweet, easy. His arms, when they hold me, seem to care, even when I can find no reassurance in his words or in his glance.

All of this is *my* reaction. In spite of Hank's brief for openness and honesty, I can only suspect what he is thinking or feeling. He doesn't say. I *know* there are still dregs of bitterness and anger in him when he tells me "You won the argument, but you're going home alone!" When I try to break through his privacy, he is funny, charming, or just plain resistant. I am close enough to see, without his telling me, that he does not have it "made." That he is putting up *his bella figura*. That many nights in his beautiful apartment with the view, he is lonely. I sense an emptiness in the apartment; it is space Hank is occupying, not living in. I am half amused, half touched by his unintentional parody on housekeeping. He was always so marvelously incompetent at home; and even now, heating and eating a frozen dinner remains remarkably complex and difficult for him.

I am often Hank's sexual partner, sometimes his friend, but I remain, always, his separated wife. When it comes to economics and other family matters, he is careful to divide "his" and "hers" in terms of costs and responsibilities. He will make suggestions when I have a problem (that time, for example, when my home insurance was canceled), help out with a telephone call or two, but he remains carefully uncommitted, segregated. "Do what you want," he will tell me. For years I desperately wanted that prerogative, but now it makes me lonely, deserted, totally responsible for myself.

Money matters inescapably come between us. We have words over the cost of Erika's new "independence" apartment, spar over the drug-store bill. Hank is scrupulous about deducting the nonmedical items before he pays the bill. He is right. But right or not, I resent his clear separation of himself from responsibility for me and my problems.

In spite of myself, I understand the resentment and frustration over money matters that Hank must be experiencing. Now that I have learned to worry about money, how to be protective—if not downright greedy—I see it through Hank's eyes. After he sends me a check, pays Erika's apartment rent and her college tuition, what's left is little more than his own rent and most basic expenses. I see him earning a living joylessly, without incentive or reward. I am uncomfortable with my part in this picture.

The time does come when I can no longer flutter and look helpless. I must take a position.

The episode begins with a note from Hank: "I don't want to be Rubinoff on his violin, but I will be facing enormous bills in September, when both girls are in college. Under the agreement, you will be receiving an unexpected additional $1,500 this year. Will you put this toward the college expense?"

Alan Springer's reaction is: "He has a nerve! The agreement clearly says he is responsible for the college bills. I'm going to call Elkan and give him hell!"

I *know* what the agreement says. What I need to know is: Is there justice in Hank's demands, justice in the agreement? If we were still living together, I would undoubtedly be contributing toward the college bills out of my earnings. I go round and round on this one, stopping now at the red, now at the black.

A part of me—the part that equates money with an end to anxiety—does not want to forgo the unexpected bonus. It looks large and luxurious. A part of me wants to be fair, however. There's no point in asking Alan whether Hank has any right on his side. Alan has one string to his bow: "Why are you afraid of what Hank thinks? Don't let him sweet-talk you. Don't let him corner you about the moral implications." Alan, of course, does not realize that Hank can sweet-talk me, can corner me, because we are lovers at the same time we are at odds over money.

I am absolutely sure that I do not want to tangle with Hank about money, that I do not want to flush conflict out into the open and put us on opposite sides. Yet I am not clear about *what* I am protecting: a man who calls me, takes me to dinner, sleeps with me, or the almost nonexistent possibility of a husband who might, who just might, come back.

I make an offer: a compromise. I will *lend* Hank the money until the girls have finished college. Then, when his expenses are radically reduced, he can return the money to me.

No, he says. He will not do it that way. His refusal is absolute. His mien is tight and cold. There is no sign whatsoever of his usual easy smile.

We reach an impasse that almost brings us to a full stop. But suddenly, for no reason I can grasp, Hank withdraws. "I will forget about it. But I want you to know that I do not feel good about this." He never mentions it again. My feelings do not still so quickly.

And now I ask myself the unavoidable questions: Why am I holding on? Is the affair with Hank—mired in habit and uncertainty—worth the dinner, the sex, and the candle? I begin to think *I* should break it off. I consider the aloneness that will result. I try to see it as a challenge. To see the advantages. I will never truly be involved with anyone else so long as I rely on Hank not only for my income but for my male companionship. I am holding *him* back, perhaps, from finding someone else. *I* think of divorce now. Separation is a meaningless status. If I break with Hank, I want to be free.

But how free can I become if I am being supported, if I am beholden?

CHAPTER XVII

Inventory

Things fall apart; the centre cannot hold; . . .
—W. B. YEATS

"COME TO dinner on June twelfth." I accept the invitation with a small grimace my friend cannot "hear" over the telephone. In my frame of mind, I do not welcome the remainder that June 12 will mark the second anniversary of separation; an anniversary that suggests inventory at a time when I am looking upon my life as half empty rather than half full, when I sense nervously that there is no longer time for me to dawdle, without direction.

And yet I *have* moved on. I can be almost disloyal to the emotions of that first year, intolerant of my own past self. I can even ask, with the detachment of an outsider: Was all that emotion really necessary? I can permit myself to remember. As I knot a blue scarf over my sweater, I think easily: "Hank always liked blue." It was part of my wife life.

The significance of the two-year mark is underlined by Jill's departure for college. She leaves for a six-week summer session at her new college in the Midwest; then she will be home only two weeks in August before going for the full academic year. Jill is following Erika out of the house into what she refers to as her "own life," leaving behind only her stuffed animals, out-of-season clothes, and marks on the walls where her posters and pictures once hung. I am alone. The last bed other than mine has been emptied.

For months I have been waiting for this critical time, not letting out my full apprehension. But the day Jill goes, I do not cry, collapse, tremble, run for shelter, or put the house up for sale. Instead, I have extra floodlights installed and burn them far more than is economical. Evenings, I turn to television and the telephone, enjoying neither, but needing to adjust to emptiness. At bedtime, my whole body listens for night sounds, trying to distinguish the friendly from the hostile. I do not completely exorcise my fears, but I bully them sufficiently to sleep through the night.

Living alone is a variable. I do not love it or hate it. I simply accommodate. I have no choice.

I counsel myself: do not attribute all problems to aloneness and separation. I am the mother of two teen-age daughters, daughter to an aging mother, and owner of far too many modern conveniences near their retirement. The drama of my own emotions, no matter how compelling, cannot isolate or immunize me from other lives, or from the demanding details of my own.

I must worry about the bills and my bank balance, remove my snow tires, run the washing machine, defrost food for supper, and remember when I am out of coffee. I must write and call Erika and Jill regularly, worry about my mother, who lives alone, and talk with friends who have *their* operations, ills, children, and problems. I must make decisions: whether to stay on my job or go back to free-lance work. I must face the surgery in the offing, and go to the dentist. It is not separation that causes me to fight constantly against letting my figure become "comfortable," that forces me to come to terms with the fact that Erika is living in an "arrangement" with Bart. These are the natural by-products of my age and stage, of a lifetime of relationships. The problems are as ongoing, as open-ended as life itself. Separation does not cause any of this. But it does affect and color my thinking, my choices, my tensions.

The central fact is that I must run my own life. When the car stalls, when a pipe springs a leak, when a porch light goes out, I must cope. I feel put-upon. A martyr.

Shot through every day is the nagging problem of money. I have inherited the shoe of responsibility from Hank, and now *I* talk about money, think about it, and worry about a possible hole in the roof or the death of one of my overage appliances. I live in dread of an unexpected major expenditure. I am still experiencing the silt of anxiety deposited by the first year; I am preoccupied, almost obsessed with the need for economic security.

But my finances *are* built on sand. I have something to worry about! Hank's new partnership is prosperous, but the dissension grows daily among the men, threatening to kill the goose that delivers my monthly golden egg. I cannot allow myself to forget that my economic existence is tied to Hank's. My own own job—if I am to believe the rumors at the coffee breaks—may soon be swept away. The fat, prosperous company for which I work has come upon lean days.

I am far better at worrying than managing. Even with two sources of income, I am constantly in a state of deficit financing. I long for the first of each month so I can get even and start afresh. Each month I vow to be more frugal, to manage better, and to save; common sense would indicate saving every possible dollar. My resolve lasts a week or two. Sometimes three. But I am impulsive, inconsistent. After a period of abstinence, I feel so virtuous I break out again with some uncontrollable expenditure. I am a money-holic. I know I should give up the house, my manner of dressing, the weekly dayworker, my openhanded gift-giving. But old ways are stubbornly rooted. The only standard of living easy to reduce, I learn, is somebody else's.

My anxiety about money has interesting side effects. Not only do I empathize with Hank's frustrations and resentments, but I can, for the first time, understand why my mother clings so anxiously to her "few securities." I do not admire it; I simply understand it. I no longer see myself as generous and nonmaterial. My attitude toward money is conditioned directly by my inner and my outer prosperity.

Yet on the surface, I am managing well—financially and otherwise. I continue to live in my charming house, to give small but elegant dinner parties, to play tennis, and to study French, mythology and folk dancing—all while holding down my job. My friends, who are a warm, supportive claque, tell me I have handled myself admirably. Remarkably. One friend, more privy to my secrets than any other since Julia, tells me, "You don't need Hank. You're happier now."

I look into the mirror my friends hold up and I see it is all a façade. A fake. Their pride in me *compels* me to be great. When I am less than great, I am ashamed to confess. I miss Julia, with whom there were no holds barred.

I cannot snow myself with my own *bella figura.* Don't they see? Something is centrally wrong. The strands of my life unwind independently, not forming a rational, discernible pattern. I fight against a moody, unsatisfied climate within, a sense of passing aimlessly through time and space. How can the friend who thinks I'm "happier"—how can she guess that what I want most is a more conventional, less diffuse existence? I am not suddenly and foolishly looking back to my marriage as the fulfillment of romantic yearnings. But I know now, even as I knew then, that I *like* being a wife. I like being with a man, doing for him; two years later, I still feel left out when I hear a man say "My wife tells me . . ." or "My wife always says . . ." That same husband may cheat, may belittle his wife's opinions publicly, may be a flop as a lover; but they are together, and I am apart. Alone.

The *idea* of aloneness still traps me. There is still fallout, still a dark part of me living under a psychological rock—the part that continues to look on, as a deprived child, at other lives gathered in the warm light of a living room. I am drawn in involuntary tropism toward the sounds, the vitality, the interconnectedness of those lives under one roof. Sense and taste hold me back. I cannot graft onto lives that are a closed circle.

I accept what friends offer but cannot make this the bread and wine of my everyday living. My family—the nuclear, biological family that is being scrutinized, criticized, and rejected by sociologists and by young people—is broken and gone. I am a refugee, displaced, without expectations. But with the insistent life force of the survivor, I am looking for resettlement. I think often of a "new life."

I am back where Hank left me originally: I, a woman, need a man.

But I look levelheadedly at the arithmetic of the situation, and it is discouraging. Men in Hank's age bracket are choosing women ten to twenty years younger. Men in public life—Governor Rockefeller, Justice Douglas, Senator Clark— are setting, or perhaps merely following, the trend. While I like men better than I ever have, and they seem to like me, I am not unlike a used car out on the lot: simply one of too many.

I am not statistical and arithmetical by inclination. I am

stubborn. I cling childishly, against facts and numbers, to the prospect, the possibility, of someone new—perhaps even the Great Romance, the Real Understanding I have been seeking all my life. I still cannot let go of the Sleeping Beauty myth. And yet, I'm afraid of a second marriage. Could I alter my habits and desires to those of some man yet unknown, to some man other than Hank? I am haunted by the specter that for the rest of my life, no matter what, the marriage to Hank will be the "real" marriage; and any other, an afterthought, a substitute, an ersatz.

My thinking becomes diffuse and contradictory, but my actions are single. As a woman alone, I am alert for signals from any attractive man—preferably unmarried; and in a discreet, well-mannered, but unmistakable way, I give off signals of my own. I am unabashedly looking.

My encounters with Cal and with Dr. Browning may not have taught me new techniques, as Hank thinks, but they have taken the seductive woman in me out of the deep freeze, leaving me vulnerable, easy to involve. I am warmed by the sun of male attention. I blush and feel arousal. I can retain some grace and self while playing sexual games. I like talking to a man. His maleness becomes part of the conversation—a sensual element, like the smell of pipe tobacco clinging to his clothes, or the size and shape of his hands, moving as we talk. The woman in me is in good working order. It is not surprising that I have experiences not possible for the wife once disinclined to adventure.

With Jill off in summer school, I decide to go to New York one day. I am empty and free, cocky and in need of assurance as I wait on the station platform in a morning of intoxicating sunshine. I smile—with only a little malice afterthought—at a tanned, athletic-looking man who holds the train door for me. As a natural consequence of my smile, and his returning smile, we sit together. I settle back with my *New York Times*. He opens *The Wall Street Journal*. By the time we pull into Pennsylvania Station, he has told me that he recently missed the brass ring in business; that he sold a five-million-dollar concern for one million; that his wife is less interested in sex than he, but that rather than upset the marriage of twenty-five years, he finds it elsewhere. He has reached a hand out to my knee, and giggled like a naughty schoolboy in a style reminiscent of the twenties!

For the next weeks, he calls persistently, insistently. When will I be going to New York again? His invitation is specific. In my need for excitement, intrigue, involvement of any kind, his suggestion moves from impossible to the realm of possible. And one afternoon I take the elevator to the twenty-third floor of the Hotel Americana to go to bed with him.

I walk down the hall with all the spontaneity of a windup toy. This is not my scene. But I hear Ben Diamond's voice in my ears: "Why not, Eve? You need some sex life besides Hank. You need some fun."

There's probably too much Russian in my nature for this kind of fun. The experience is an ungarnished act of sex, as pedestrian and tasteless as the room in the midday glare. The man begins to undress at once; to undress me. I don't want to be here. I should walk out. But I cannot face the awkwardness. I have let it come this far, to the point of no return. I stay. In the bed, he performs like a sixteen-year-old, with little knowledge of, and less skill with, the female anatomy; he is in a hurry to care for his own needs, and I am a convenience in the bed, much as I have always imagined a prostitute to be. I think: "No wonder his wife is not interested!" Throughout the act—happily brief—I am conscious of my age and my surgical scars as I have been with no other man.

Afterward, we talk, and he tells me how to save money on my income tax! He is more at ease in these few minutes than in the act of intercourse. In truth, so am I. He gets out of bed abruptly, puts on his shorts, and begins to make business calls. I take this as my signal to dress and leave. I am relieved to be out in the street, out in the open air, among anonymous crowds. I drop the episode from my mind. It is a shoddy piece of clothing I bought—thinking it a bargain. I have no guilt. Only distaste, and relief that no one need know. I vow: "No more junk!"

I next try to fabricate some sexuality, some attraction in a man who has none for me. On a midsummer weekend, I fly to Nantucket with Jeremy Bergman, a conventional bright man who, at fifty-four, has never married, and has the un-alterable habits of a maiden lady. Jeremy is ill at ease with women, yet pursues them, and needs their companionship. I've seen him a dozen times, in the style of my girlhood dating days, always uncertain whether I want to go another time. But during the weekend, I bask in the protective luxury of having a man to carry the luggage, arrange reservations, pick up the check at mealtime. I insist upon separate rooms, but we walk, swim, hold hands, and kiss sweetly in the summer sun. Jeremy blossoms with the sea air and the holi-day setting. I see him in a new way. And I even fancy myself falling in love with the same man I was half loath to be with only a few weeks earlier. But Sunday evening as we thread through the crowds at Kennedy Airport, my male Cinderella turns back into a pumpkin—all that is left of the weekend is a fresh coat of tan!

And next I try going backward in time. On a day when I

am disconsolate and restless, I impulsively look up the address of R.B.—the *first* R.B., the ghost lover of my marriage. I send him a brief note: Wouldn't it be interesting to meet again after all these years? It is over twenty years since I last saw him; but in all that time I have, in secret recess, given him the unstinting adoration and respect I scanted Hank. R.B. was an odd one who sat next to me in graduate school. At first I was annoyed when he passed notes to me during class, commented on my looks and my dress during the lectures. But in time I came to love his oddness, to savor his clipped upper-class speech, his extravagant opinions, his way of laughing loudly at himself and the foibles of a foibled world. His eyes, behind great dark-rimmed glasses, invited and mocked women—all women, pretty and dowdy, brazen and shy. I was fascinated by a man so fascinated by women.

His reply to my note comes immediately, on thick ecru stationery embossed in brown. He suggests meeting for a drink when I am next in New York.

On the day of our appointment, I go to an expensive hairdresser, pack a chiffon nightgown, and register at a luxury hotel. As I wait for him in the sedate University Club, I am filled with memories of our time together at school, of the night I went with him to the St. Regis Hotel. I remember, too, the day he told me he had just been married. I closed the door to my office that afternoon and cried as I typed.

"Eve!" His voice is exactly the same, sending reverberations through the genteel quiet, and reminding my senses. He leans down to kiss me with obvious pleasure, and the twenty odd years drop away, to the camaraderie of a college reunion.

He is married for the second time, and assures me I'd enjoy Louise, his new wife. She is fifteen years younger than he is. He's sorry, after an hour, that he must leave for dinner. He did not realize I would be in town for the evening. "Call me when you come again. We'd like you to come up to the apartment."

I go back to my hotel room and the chiffon nightgown. For the rest of the evening I watch television. I never do meet Louise, and, oddly, I stop thinking about R.B.—except now and then, when I wonder whether he has really settled down.

I've heard other women without men say it's not worth going out just to go out; that they'd rather be at home reading or watching television. I suspect they are sincere—*after* the fact, when an evening has been dull or a downright failure. But for myself, I hold stubbornly to anticipation and to the enabling proposition that all things are possible. I go each time I am asked, because I am still optimistic. I might find something I need, something that is missing from my life. I do not allow myself to be humiliated—at least not for long—by those times that end grotesquely. I am not a virginal young girl, giving up her hymen in a sacred ritual. If, in my enthusiasm and optimism, I am trying to will intimacy and warmth into these random episodes, I still come away each time with knowledge of another kind of man, as well as some new knowledge of myself. In an odd way, I look upon the men in these two years with a sense of accomplishment—as I do upon the money I earned. I have no money left; the men do not last. But just as the job adds to my confidence and to the backlog of social security payments, if not to my savings account, so the men add—in another way—to my knowledge of men. I find it possible to learn from "cheap" experiences, even as I often find some wisdom, some insight in the pages of a "cheap" novel.

I finally lose the girlish notion that all sex is exciting. I find that physical, like human, encounters fall short of perfection. And yet the needs are still deep. I yearn for warmth and attention. The aftermath—the quiet lying together in intimacy—is still far sweeter, far more nourishing to the woman in me than the act itself.

Triggered by my nothing-to-lose attitude, I have unwittingly become part of the sexual revolution. All conventional morality bombed out. No barriers to any bed—except wish and will. When a clerk in a shoe store asks, "Do you fuck?" or when a drunk says to me, "I'd like to get inside your pants," how can I take offense as an innocent when I am, in truth, experienced?

CHAPTER XVIII

Turnaround

If I am not for myself, who will be for me? And
if I am only for myself, what am I? And if not
now, when?
— HILLEL

"THERE HAS been a change. You must have surgery
immediately—for your protection!" I am in the office of the
specialist, a medical high lama. I have come for a routine
checkup, expecting his usual reminder that I must have
surgery some time "soon." He has abruptly removed the
illusion of choice.

Reflexly, I find a telephone booth and call Hank. "Where
are you?" he asks. "I'll meet you there in ten minutes." He
buys me a drink at the nearest hotel bar, encourages me
to cry, offers to spend the afternoon with me. I am grateful
for his support, and lean hard.

But with the tears over, I become strangely calm. Not
maudlin, not agitated. I am almost relieved to cease shadow-
boxing with fear, to have the decision made for me. I know
from my previous hospital experience how alone I will be;
the aloneness seems more critical to me than the physical act

of surgery. No one, not Hank or the children, not the warmest of friends, not Ben Diamond, can alleviate *this* aloneness.

I get ready for the hospital, severing myself from the outside world. I am not protesting, not fighting, not feeling sorry for myself. I resolve to get it over with as quickly, as quietly as possible. To face whatever it will bring with an acceptance I have never before been capable of.

"You're fine . . . do you hear, Eve? It's over, and you're fine!" Hank is trying to reach me through the haze of anesthesia. It is too much effort to open my eyes, to speak. I lapse back, and feel rather than see Erika wiping my forehead with a damp, cold cloth, telling me "You were just great, Mom, great!" I am dimly aware, when I wake again, that Hank is sprawled in the easy chair near the bed.

The surgery goes better than anyone could have hoped for. My recovery is ahead of its own timetable. In forty-eight hours, I am practicing the deep breathing I learned in yoga class and demanding solid food. Hank is attentive enough in the hospital—calling, visiting. It may be only in my mind, but I sense a missing element that would make *his* concern different from that of any good friend. The missing element is responsibility. I resent it. But I accept it. I am determined to see myself through the recovery, as I have through the surgery, as though I were alone in the world.

Afterward, I am euphoric with relief. I am buoyed up by the success, by a sudden knowledge that I have met this test, as well as the test of living alone, with more strength than I knew I possessed. It is an exhilarating sensation. I fill out my skin more proudly, walk more surely, even for those first tentative steps down the hospital corridor. I own myself. I feel Hank carried along by my mood. He is enthusiastic about my foolproof recovery. In a moment of ugly suspicion,

I wonder if he is relieved that I am not going to be even more of a dependent!

Hank takes me to dinner for the first time since the hospital. I am high on being out. At the restaurant, we are seated next to Dr. Adam Donald, a brilliant moody man we've known for many years. We know his wife. We know his children. But we do not know the woman he is with—a delicate, pretty blond woman in her early thirties. We are so surprised at finding Adam with another woman that we are trapped into pretending we do *not* see him—six feet away. Once we have taken our parts in this little comedy, we cannot retreat. I am facing their table, and it is impossible not to see and sense the animation and sparkle with which the woman is leaning forward to catch Adam's words, not to know that he is feeling expansive and pleasured with her.

I do not feel judgmatic. I think: "That's the way it is. A moody, restless man like Adam—it's inevitable." I catch myself. If I am not judgmatic about Adam, why didn't I take the same attitude about Hank? Hank and Leslie must have had just such intense, flirtatious conversations when they were first together.

Dinner is too long. I feel the tiredness of convalescence, which comes on as swiftly as a summer storm. I feel pale under my make-up. I need a haircut. After Hank leaves, I cannot sleep. As I try one side of the bed, then the other, I see Adam and the girl. I wonder: "What can habit, time, long togetherness offer that competes with the champagne of discovery, of freshness? What does a *wife* have to offer? What do *I* have to offer?" I fall asleep only when I find a partial answer: offer him back the part of himself he has invested in me!

In the aftermath of surgery, I feel a new warmth, a fresh

acceptance from Hank. The mood changes. He drops his small, carping themes about my lack of honesty, my inability to be free. I sense a subtle but definite shift between us.

I can feel it when it happens—on a specific Saturday night.

Something new, or perhaps something old, comes into the relationship through a back door, through an evening that might easily have ended otherwise. I call Hank that Saturday morning, and he answers grumpily, "I'm not up yet!" My woman's radar detects that this is not the cocoon of sleep, but the eye of a depressive storm.

"I suppose you called early so I could invite you to dinner?"

"Well—are you asking?" I can never forgo the flirtatious habit, or a Saturday night out.

I suggest we go out into the country as a change. I want to break the pattern of starting in Hank's apartment, where we might easily go round in an all-too-familiar circle.

On the drive, Hank is subdued, not talkative, but with the first drink he becomes more open, more at ease—and his troubles come tumbling out. We talk and talk, through the steak, through the coffee and the brandy. About his depressions. He is more honest, more forthright with me than he has ever been. We talk about whether he should try therapy once more. We talk about the threatening breakup in the office and its impact on Hank's disturbed mood.

The evening is one of our best. I feel ground under my feet. This is not the boy-girl game that we have played so long, but that is beginning to pall on me. I feel no less desirable, no less womanly in Hank's eyes, or in my own, because we have turned to real problems. I am his friend who listens, the wife who is not a wife.

Until tonight I was telling myself that our lives were linked only economically, that I was moving out emotionally. But now as I sit here, I am no longer certain. I am thinking and feeling about what Hank is telling me, not simply listening. I try to examine *my* motives as suspiciously as I did Hank's. Am I supporting him through the crisis so he can support me—financially? I think of a more subtle, menacing possibility: that when Hank is in trouble, I am more at ease, more in command of the situation. But it is also possible that Hank has changed. It is possible that Hank has learned about himself, and that *I* have learned to look upon depression as a widespread endemic problem, not simply as Hank's individual weakness.

As I listen and talk, talk and listen, I do not mirror back Hank's depression with an uncertainty of my own, as I so often did when we were "married." I am *separate* from Hank, which enables me to look upon the depression as his, not as an assault on my own overguarded inner fortress.

When we get back to the house, Hank comes in, the first time he has spent alone with me in the house since he walked out. We are at ease, involved. Serious, but laughing—sometimes just quiet. We stretch out on the floor in front of the fireplace, prop our feet up on the couch. We talk about change. Do I think he has changed? Does he think I have? Can we change if we want to? Hank assures me: "There are some things you shouldn't change. Some things are great. Just great."

The next morning, that evening is still with me. Not a wild, passionate thing—but a good calm. I hope Hank feels the same. I know it is from that evening on that I sense the ground rules changing, a hurrying toward conclusiveness that was not in the evenings which went before.

If Hank is in the neighborhood now, he stops in: "Hello, hello. Anybody home?" On one such brief stop, Geraldine, who has lived alongside so many of our years, is in the kitchen ironing. She does not look up when I fix lunch for

Hank, does not show surprise. She says in a stage whisper: "Maybe you'll take him back. He's a *good* man"—pause— "but there's something wrong with all of them!"

There are more evenings in front of my fireplace, more talk about business problems, about us. Hank is no longer tense about being a "guest." He seems to enjoy the small suppers I put together hastily. I suspect he is thoroughly wearied of restaurant meals. He puts his feet up, leaves his familiar trail of burned-out matches as he smokes his pipe.

We begin to be seen publicly—at the theater and concerts, at more popular dinner places. I ask, a bit coyly: "Are you sure you want to be seen with me?" He replies brusquely: "Isn't the answer obvious?" Of course I am asking other questions: Do *I* want to be seen with Hank? Do *I* want to commit myself? I do not know whether Hank knows yet. But I know. It is so patent, I don't even need intuition. He's thinking of coming back!

And now it is I who am complex, unpredictable, full of twists, turns, and surprises. I have done everything a woman could do. I have come to terms with my part in the angry dialogue that ended our marriage. I have shrugged off Hank's outright rejection, and then the quasi rejection of his take-it-or-leave-it attitude. I would have no truck with the nonsense of my pride. I made overture after overture. I stood by while Hank's hostility literally reversed itself into good will, and now that he is within touching distance, I go cold. I suddenly cannot face the decision I suspect I must soon make.

I am getting ready to go to Vermont for the last stage of my convalescence, to walk in the pine woods, to sleep with my window flung open to the clear, sharp autumn air.

Hank comes to dinner the night before I leave. I wear a bright-red pants suit with a soft white blouse. "You look wonderful," he says, as he kisses me hello. "You know, I have nothing but the warmest feelings for you." I accept the words lightly, graciously, but I know what is coming.

He is abrupt and restless during dinner; afterward, he clears away the small talk. "I want to discuss the possibility of our living together. I assume that you want this." These are his exact words, stiff, heavy with the embroidery of his pride. This is the man who said, more than two years ago, "I am a proud and stubborn man. Once I walk out that door, I will not come back."

It is the pride I hear when he lists his "conditions."

"I want to be Number One.

"I want to live in an apartment in town. We can live in mine until we find a larger one.

"You cannot move in a stick of furniture that I do not approve of—except in your room." I am to have a bedroom of my own.

"You are free to do what you want. I will do what I want."

And the last article of the proposition: "Your friends are nice people, but they do not interest me. I do not want to see them, but you can see them without me."

I cannot, after more than a year, say, "This is so sudden." Nor can I laugh, even a little, at his proposition, put forward like some carefully thought-out deal. I do not take umbrage. I know so well that Hank is protecting himself; the self for which he has been fighting so hard; for which, in part, he walked out on the marriage.

"React," Hank demands as I am silent with my own thoughts. "I wish I could know what's inside your head."

No he doesn't! If I were "honest," revealing, I suspect he would walk out of the house forever. I hide the "real" questions that beset me and fill the space with practical questions about apartment living, about the problem of Hank's depressions.

I have enough openness, enough freedom remaining to bring up some fundamental issues.

"I want to be wanted . . ."

"Why do you think I asked you?" is his reply.

"If we fall back into the old ways, I couldn't bear it. I couldn't live through that again."

"That's behind us," he says.

"We ought to go together, try it out," I tell him.

He smiles. "That's not real. I suggest that when you come back from Vermont, you come down and live in the apartment for a month. That will be a more meaningful test."

But he leaves no doubt that my decision must be made soon. "Don't make yourself hard to get, or I won't want it." He does not have to add, since I already know: "I have my pride."

I find myself numb, a reaction I have had all my life to the moments that demand the most emotion. I am not so numb that I do not call two friends before I leave the next morning. Perhaps there is triumph, vindication: See, I can do it! I did it! He wants me back!

"Do what is best for *you*. I know how hard it must be to live alone," says one friend. The other tells me, "I hope you *do* go back. I think it is better. I see that you are not going to marry again so fast . . ."

CHAPTER XIX

Decision Making

. . . the individual has no recourse from the
necessity of making final decisions for himself—
and to make them, in the last analysis, in freedom and isolation may require literally as well
as figuratively an agony of anxiety and inward
struggle.

—ROLLO MAY

O N   M Y way to Vermont the next day, I drive too fast. But
I cannot outrun the task, the tension of decision. I told
Hank I would "think it over"—and I do. Morning, noon,
and night. I am not at ease. I am a Klee portrait cleft into
parts, wanting to be unified, decided, at peace.

It is not an orderly process of asking myself whether I do
or do not want to go back to Hank. I walk for hours along
the wooded paths, a roiling, boiling cauldron of doubts,
fears, ideas, all contradictory, confounding, exhausting. I
think of nothing else. The Question is inescapable. Everything I read, hear, say, leads me to ask, over and over: Should
I go back?

I wait for a resolution that does not come. Instead, my

mind, invited to choose, presents, as I walk, even as I sleep, fragments, short essays, arguments, homilies, flashbacks. Each is remarkably clear while I am thinking it. Yet, often as not, contradictory to what my mind offered only an hour before. In the process, I uncover enough insights for a year or two more of psychoanalysis. But no decision. No stage directions for action. I am still convinced the decision exists, hiding within me. I do not want to write an ending, I want it to "happen," as Lillian Hellman describes it in *An Unfinished Woman:* "I awake, feeling my head is made of sand, and that a pole has just been pulled from it with the end of the pole carrying a card on which there is an answer to a problem, clearly solved and set out as if it has been arranged for me on a night table." Meanwhile, I look for the pieces of myself everywhere—in Hank's eyes, in the eyes of my friends, in my work—all the while exhorting the *real* Eve to stand up!

One of the more exquisite tortures is that the doubt is reminiscent of my sudden doubt those last days before my wedding. Again, I do not know whether I am disregarding an important signal or whether it is my nature to balk at the barrier, like a skittish horse!

I am not deciding. I am indecision. I scold myself, tell myself I am practicing the problem, not the solution; that there must be a more level way to resolve an issue, without this chaos, this confusion at the center of my being. I even try making two lists: what I have to gain, what I have to lose. I come up with two remarkably frank lists—but no decision.

Hank calls after dinner, and the widow who runs the inn says, "He sounds solicitous and nice. They don't make them like that anymore!" After her years alone, she is hungry for the thought and concern she hears in that call.

As I walk along the evening road, my mind leaps at our being together, at the company, the shelter, the end of irresolution. I think it is sensible and right to go back. We have honed each other to our particular ways through the years. How can I *not* go back! I will no longer be scrabbling for a man, coveting other women's husbands—more as husbands than as lovers! I plan. If Hank wants an apartment in town, I will find a small seashore house where I can go when I need to be in touch with the sun and the sky. Thinking of the seashore house, I wonder: "Will I be free to come and go? To make such decisions about my time? About myself?"

Suddenly I become suspicious, not trusting the freedom Hank has promised. He means it, when he says it, but I'm not sure that freedom of this sort *is* compatible with marriage. I want too much. Is any man, especially Hank, willing to give this much in a conventional marriage? I think of other, far more important freedoms that may be jeopardized. Am I the classic instance of a freed bird compulsively returning to the cage with its door still open? When the "honeymoon" period is over, will we trap each other once again with the same demands, needs, resentments? In this framework, it is easy to dwell on ways in which Hank is not lovable, to remind myself that Hank can be moody, cantankerous, tyrannizing through unreason. How will I comply with what seem to me his unreasonable requests? Easily, perhaps, the first few times; then more reluctantly, more annoyedly; with Hank getting annoyed in counterreaction. I am ill with the premonition that it will end where it ended before. What a fool I am to let it come this far . . .

In another while, with another random thought to change my direction, I come full circle: yes, I *should* go back.

Two years ago, a year ago, even as recently as six months ago, I wanted this. Why am I now undergoing the agony of indecision? Have I changed? Moved on? Have we lost the thread together? Why, now, am I dwelling on Hank's flaws when I have learned that this *is* my flaw?

I come back to love. In an effort to be forthright, not to trap myself again in my own guilt, I even approach this with Hank: ask him if affection, loyalty, concern will be enough for him. But "love" opens the door on old, dark places, leads me down winding corridors to myself, to the source of the turmoil. What I now experience is more sadness than guilt. I think less that I am cheating Hank at this stage, more about what I have missed by not loving.

Once I have looked into the darkest, most forbidding places, I am free to ask: What is wrong with returning to a man for companionship, and my own good reasons? In an attempt to escape the compulsion to love that has been laid upon me by a culture of love, I marshal to my side such people as Margaret Mead, who says: "Love is the invention of a few high cultures. . . . in terms of a personal, highly intense choice, it is a cultural artifact. . . ." And again: "To make love the requirement of a lifelong marriage is exceedingly difficult, and only a very few people can achieve it." And La Rochefoucauld, who says "most people, if they had not heard of love, would not be in love." But they do not convince me. The trouble is: I do not want to disbelieve in romantic love. I want to be capable of it! I want to believe there is "true love" as well as affection and used-to-ness. But if I believe in it, I must then see myself as shut out of this paradise!

Through the labyrinth of my thoughts, I do not completely trust myself. Like the Russians in Koestler's *Darkness at Noon*, I have the capacity for confessing sins I have not committed. Why do I feel at ease in Hank's arms? Why do I have a sense of place with him? My place! Why do I like to have him make much of me, to be concerned about me? Why do I step back so quickly, so naturally, into the role of wife? I know this much: many another woman, with all this going for her, would *convince* herself that she loved Hank; would accept him, accept her acceptance, and give them both her blessings! If I were to stop my self-inquisition, I might find this is what I want!

And what about Hank? Not the Hank who exists in my mind, but the three-dimensional Hank with his own flesh-and-blood temperament. Why does *he* now want to come back to me? I do not worry about whether he loves me. I accept the fact that he wants me, needs me and what I can offer—the companionship, the support, the wifely services. On that score, I am altogether content and unquestioning. Is his side of the coin, in fact, any different from mine?

I am drawn out of the taut circle of my thinking, the mishmash of emotion and ideas, by circumstances.

Hank calls to tell me his dad has been taken to the hospital. In another twenty-four hours, when the medical confusion clears, we learn that his father has cancer. Operation is no longer possible. He becomes comatose.

In this same period, Hank is fighting for his financial existence. After the months of dissension, the business is about to split apart. Hank is beset. I hear it in his voice. I offer to come back for a few days if he wants someone to talk to, someone to listen. I do not consider myself altruistic. At the very least, my economic future is at stake along with his. Hank accepts instantly, adding that of course he'll meet me at the airport, that he will pay my plane fare.

We call back and forth about planes, meetings, and Hank says, "You'll have to make some decisions while you're here."

I back away. "I can't make them that fast."

"You may have to."

I hear coolness in the short silence.

"Don't get unfriendly signals," I tell him—I *have* learned some new ways in the years between. I do not put up an instant barrier of my own. I talk, fill the empty space, deflect the small crisis.

But I am not as calm as I sound. I volunteered. I want to go. But I grow numb with the pressure to decide quickly. When I become numb, I am out of touch with my inner chaos. I remind myself sternly that it is *my* decision; that I cannot allow myself to be pressured, to be swayed. That it is *my* life I am deciding! I am the echo of every teen-ager taking a stand for independence, while yearning for someone stronger, surer, wiser to provide the answers and the decisions.

I spend an important few days at home with Hank. We talk and talk; about Hank's dad, about problems in the business. We are at ease. And I am learning to be more open, to bring out the child who hid under the blankets to cry, who carried her unhappiness off to solitude, like some form of mental masturbation. The more open I become with Hank, the more I like him! And the more I like him, the more open I can be! It is a self-fulfilling cycle. I urge him not to press me for a decision. Decision means change, and I know now that I am not good at change.

Before I return to Vermont, we stop at the hospital; we drive out into the country for lunch; we go to bed together— it is warm, friendly, but Hank is having impotence problems. We are able to talk about this, too! Here, as in the matter of depression, I know more; know it can be any man's problem, not just Hank's. In truth, I want to be held, want to be wanted, as much as anything. Hank takes me to the airport on Sunday, handles my ticket, my luggage, treats me with a gallantry I have had in small doses only from other women's husbands. While I am trying to outguess the future, we are forming more and more connective tissues.

I am back two days later when I receive an emergency telephone call. Hank's father has died.

Hank acts as though I were doing him some immense favor when I come down for the funeral, but it would be my obligation, I know, if we were still estranged. Jill flies in from college and arrives at the airport fifteen minutes after me. Erika comes with Hank to meet us. There are four of us in the small business of getting the luggage, the car, driving into town. The first time in almost two years. We have dinner together, and in spite of the knowledge of death, it is a momentous, almost festive evening. I sit next to Hank, feeling protected by his concern, knowing that he is pleased I have come—and yet I feel the four separatenesses. A family, like a marriage, is not easy to put together again. I am not quite at ease with Jill and Erika in the reunion. I am, oddly, more like a second wife making a first appearance with the husband's children of a former marriage. I am concerned, even defensive, about what they think. By coming together with Hank, after all that has happened, do they find me disloyal to their loyalty?

When we are alone, I tell Jill I am considering returning to Hank. She smiles. "That's interesting." She is very grown-up. Later, she tells me in a letter that "I am glad to see that the new serial, *The Private Lives of Eve and Hank*, is coming to an end. I knew it had to—all it takes is time."

Erika smiles, equally grown-up, and uses the same word: "Interesting." But she is more complex. "It's your decision," she says, "your business. You do what you want. . . ." I don't want to think she cares less, but that she has moved farther along in her own life. For a year she has been pulling apart and coming together with Bart in an eerie mirroring of my uncertain liaison with Hank. I've grown accustomed to their breakups and to her announcements that "Bart and I are going to try again." Much as Ben Diamond must have grown used to hearing me say, "I'm seeing Hank again."

I sit next to Hank during the funeral service, ride with him to the cemetery, and afterward serve coffee and cake to family and friends who come to the apartment. We are so obviously "friendly" that I amuse myself wondering what people are saying. Do they think it mere form, to fit the circumstance? For myself, I am supremely comfortable. I want to be here. I belong.

The next day I suggest to Hank that we drive down to the seashore to have a day alone before I return to the country. We are subdued, caught up in the death. Yet it is a golden day. As we drive, the silences are resting places for both of us. I skip along the beach. I walk with my arm in Hank's. I have been here before; but I did not know—until I did not have it—how good so simple a pleasure could be. We are companionable. We read. Talk. Look at a beach house I might want to buy. Nothing in me is fighting against Hank, or the direction I am taking.

The decision cannot be withheld much longer. By being with Hank, I am being led—I am leading him to take my acceptance for granted. We agree at the airport that we will meet in Boston the next weekend.

Back in Vermont, Hank is with me: his views, his feelings, his needs, fill my thoughts, just as his hostility and bitterness lived with me when we first parted. "Am I," I wonder, "nothing more than litmus paper, responding to light and dark, happiness and unhappiness imposed upon me?"

When I am alone again, doubts and questions stunned by the actuality of being with Hank struggle to life again. Even a middle-aged Jewish princess retreats slowly. But I have gone too far to draw back; I feel my choice becoming a nonchoice. I fight the nagging sense that I am giving up something. It defies facts and common sense. I am giving up fifty-seven varieties of loneliness for companionship, caring, protectiveness. But I am tense again, distrustful, lying in wait for the drawbacks, the disadvantages to re-emerge and say "I told you so!"

My decision does not come. I must superimpose it on indecision. When I go to Boston to meet Hank, I carry my wedding ring, which I have never thrown away.

CHAPTER XX

Accepting Acceptance

To be emotionally committed to somebody is very difficult, but to be alone is impossible. To commit is to live, and not to commit is to be dead . . .

—STEPHEN SONDHEIM, COMPOSER-
LYRICIST OF *Company*

I AWAKE early in my own house. It is the morning I plan to "move" to Hank's apartment. I lie in bed saying good-by to my room, to the stocky beech tree at the window that has leafed and unleafed through so much of my living.

I have only two choices, I now see clearly. I am free to try out living with Hank or free to live alone—chancing whatever may happen.

I lie back and accept the decision I literally superimposed upon my indecision. The acceptance opens a door, allows me to walk through to a serenity. It is like no tranquilizer I have ever experienced! I begin to see a new way of thinking. I have been digging deeper and deeper within me for The Answer. But what is important is not which choice I make; it is my acceptance of that choice, once it has been made.

My morning mindlessness tells me there *is* a bond between Hank and me, whether or not we choose to honor it. I have a moment of recognition: all the while I thought I was re-involving Hank, it was *myself* I reinvolved. What do my actions tell me that the merry-go-round in my mind will not? As I stare at the whitewash blue of the bedroom walls, I have a strong, warm impulse to accept what *is* between us; to foster it, breathe upon it, cherish it, keep it alive. If I look sidewise for a something more, a something else, I will—like Lot's wife—turn to stone.

We know our needs now. This, as much as anything, has brought us together. Hank, for all *his* bravado and bachelor life, has been at odds, floating free; and now, as he himself confesses: "I do not want to die alone." He has missed, if he could admit it, the caretaking, the structure of side-by-side existence that he once rejected as mundane, unexciting. I, too, want back what I took for granted—until I no longer had it.

What we are attempting to do is not easy. To put together two people who failed each other more than once. I think of other couples who have come back together, who cover so much with their laconic phrases—"We're working at it." "We're trying!" There are traps, risks, well-grounded fears. Hank is still stubborn, still defending as though I were attacking, while I am still fighting for myself as part of that first fight for survival in the embattled household of my childhood.

There is always the possibility that we will betray these old selves by a trigger-quick reaction that escapes precaution and the sieve of thought.

But how will we know till we try what can change? What has changed? We *think* we have changed direction, perspective, and the indefinable aura in which we move. We are generating good will as automatically as we once generated hostility. Hank says: "The break was a good thing. Good for both of us." I take this as his enabling clause, *his* door to acceptance. But I like to tease, and say to him, "This will be my *second* marriage." He replies, "The hell it is!"

For once in my life, I am supporting, not sabotaging my choice. Not that I change spots altogether. I still entertain the possibility that my new "thinking" may be nothing more than the rationalization of my choice. I still worry the future, shake it, gnaw it, as my poodle does his faded old bed pillow. But I have interesting evidence of change. If Jung is right, that we can make sense of our dreams for ourselves, I have a significant bonus as I come to terms with Hank, with my willingness to go back. I dream about my father, dead more than five years. In my dreams, my image of him is kindlier, warmer, friendlier. I see him in a new way; without so much temper and anger. I see his intense desire to live, his love of luxury—both of which I have inherited. I see him puzzled and unhappy with the "lady" he married, but indulgent and adoring of me. My picture of my past is shifting. I no longer need to feel quite so sorry for myself; to dwell on the "sins of the fathers," visiting them upon myself.

That afternoon, I go down to the apartment.

In less than a day, I am a housekeeper, sending out the laundry and cleaning, shopping for food, cooking for Hank in a kitchen with one pot, one pan, and a can opener. I move, without conscious thought, through the familiar chores of making the bed, emptying ashtrays, tidying the great piles of newspapers, magazines, mail—and removing Hank's shoes from the middle of the living-room floor. I arrange fresh flowers in an empty juice jar. After dinner, we leaf through the evening paper, trading the front and back sections companionably. We take my faithful poodle for a walk so he can sniff out his new surroundings. We are remarkably relaxed, at ease, although we are aware of ourselves, watching ourselves.

In the morning I look over at Hank in the bed. I know him. I am an instant wife. He wakes; he is glad to see me, and I am glad to be here. I hurry into the bathroom ahead of him so I can have time to fix his breakfast. It is an old happening. We have done all this before.

I am still free to stay or to go. Hank is forthright; he does not act as though it were cut and dried, preordained. Erika wants a secondhand sewing machine for her birthday. Hank and I discuss it, agree that it is a good present. We give her the gift together, and Hank tells her it is from "maybe-us." His clauses are subjunctive, conditional. He says more than once, "If it works out." I am drawn toward him, happy because he holds a loose rein. I am particularly impressed with his attitude toward the agreement; he understands that it can be looked upon as an escape valve.

I visit Alan Springer to discuss the technicalities of the situation—but not without telling Hank first that I am going. "Of course," he says, "you have to protect yourself in case it doesn't work out."

Alan Springer's viewpoint is as loose-jointed as his build. "Everything works out for the best. What will be will be. Just don't be in a hurry. You've developed a lot of inner strength." He means, I think, that living alone no longer frightens me; that I am able to give up my need to depend, to lean, if the cost of that leaning is more than I can afford to pay.

The mechanics of the matter are simple: a clause added to

the original agreement, which will say that if the attempted reconciliation does not work out, the agreement remains in force.

"Sure, it's fine with me," Hank says. "Have Alan draft the clause and send it to my lawyer."

I tell Hank that "I never again want to be a woman without money of my own." He agrees that if we sell the house I am to have half the money. In an environment of willingness and ease, the law is no longer a hostile force, money is no longer the contest. These become the extensions, the instruments of our wishes!

We have our small nonidylls. One is in bed. Hank holds onto my head as he indicates his desires, and I snap: "Don't do that!" It is a self-revealing instant. I thought I had grown more sophisticated with experience. Hank is taken aback by my sharp response. "I won't—but just tell me." The incident is gone.

We have another. I hand Hank the day's mail for his attention. "Here are the tickets for Thursday. Better put them away." He looks up at me with a grin and salutes: "Yes, sergeant!" He finds my tone commanding. I thought it emphatic. I wonder if the small incidents are significant, but I recognize that small, new problems refer back, all too quickly, to the past. My emotions are slow learners.

We have a more subtle, disturbing new problem. Hank insists that I confide in him about my sexual experiences while we were apart. He considers it part of being "open" with each other. I do not want to tell him more than I told him originally—as a tease, to make myself more marketable in Hank's eyes. To say more goes against my every instinct. I agree with the Russian writer Ilya Ehrenburg, who wrote: "I have always viewed it as a good Russian custom that two people who share a bed do not talk about it . . ." I am neither modern nor casual about sex. Is this my hang-up, as Hank insists? Ben counsels me to do as I believe, even if my values are out of fashion. "Eve, you have to be who you are. And Hank has to accept you or it won't work. He'll become more arbitrary, and you'll get sick." I finally tell Hank that there are parts of me I cannot share, that must remain private. He says I am wrong; but after a quick steam of importance, the whole matter evaporates.

I have other problems—with myself. I accept Hank and our arrangement with a lovely content for long stretches in the living room, in the bedroom, on the street. Then unbidden doubts, skepticism, nonacceptance arise. I dare not share these with Hank, who once told me, "If you have doubts, forget the whole thing!" After all my fine insights and lectures to myself, I am guilty again. Guilt is a habit. I worry: Will it presage a rerun of failure?

But I have learned to catch myself in the act. A part of me will always challenge, will always be restless, critical of myself *and* of Hank. The serenity of acceptance is not a fixed gift. It must be wooed, summoned, waited for, again and again.

We are attending the wedding of Jennifer Borden—Julia and John's older daughter—when I have one of my regressions. Jennifer has always been a soft-spoken, reflective child, and special to me. During the wedding service she turns her sweet, serious face up to Brian, her husband-to-be. Through the density of people, the expensive clothes, the perfume, Jennifer's adoration of Brian is an inner spring: a clear, sparkling freshet. Her eyes are upon him, but we are admitted in the moment of the ceremony to the private circle of her unsullied, unconditional love. The arthritis of our middle-aged affections is unstiffened and warmed. I am envious. Sharply. Physically envious. Not of Jennifer's youth and beauty—but of missing this. "This" is her adoration of him. I want so much to know the feeling for myself. There is no way to edit my thinking. I will continue to be a romantic by sublimation. But in the mood of the moment, I am restless, less pleased with Hank. The mood passes, and we move into the swell and sound of the reception.

The afternoon is my first appearance with Hank in a private setting, and our opportunity to make an unprinted announcement that we are "seeing" each other. Everyone genuinely *likes* our coming together again. They think it's "nice"; they're "glad—you always seemed to belong together." It's as though some old-fashioned virtue has triumphed, just as it does in the happy-ending movies we now see only in "camp" movies on *The Late Late Show*.

After the Borden wedding, people quickly become accustomed to seeing Hank and me together. It is no longer necessary to make small, explanatory comments. The curiosity and novelty are passing, as surely as the curiosity and interest about the original separation passed.

We are going along evenly, easily; but I do not have time to find out how well the emotions will wear. Our testing time is cut short. With surprising swiftness, Hank and his partners get a "divorce" and Hank accepts an offer of a new job in California. It is a hurried, busy time, with last-minute details of the business un-merger and Hank's move to the West Coast.

It is decided. I will follow Hank out in six weeks, when he has settled into the job and found a place to live.

We have one Battle before he leaves, very small in the telling, but large in the happening. Hank forgets to buy something I'd asked him to buy. Actually, it is a loaf of health bread at a shop he passes daily. I am irritated because he forgets. He is irritated by my irritation. And we're off. Words. More words. Counterwords. Silence. The old techniques: accusation, self-defense, counteraccusation, and the ame around another time.

"I will not let myself be upset," I say to him, self-righteously. "I will not go backward. If we cannot work out such small things, we'll never make it." I use brave words. But once the words are out, try to find a way to stop the cycle. I cannot overcome the burden of my overpowering self-justification; cannot break through to what I had hopefully believed was a larger, wiser self. I don't think I'm wrong. I don't want to apologize—because I wouldn't mean it. Hank is cold. A stone wall.

The next morning, Hank is demonstrably, showily cheerful with his good morning, but I get there first: "I'm sorry. Sorry I couldn't find a way out last night." He smiles. He was beginning to make *his* overture. I think: "Both of us are hurrying to put this incident away, to forget the words we said. We now have too much at stake."

We are committed to going back. Only with the final commitment, only when it exists, when it IS, will we learn whether we can bring some measure of relaxation and contentment to each other, whether we have been honed down for our last future, or whether, sadly, we will speed toward a conclusion I sometimes manufacture out of my secret doubts and fears. It is, as Robert Frost says:

> We dance round in a ring and suppose,
> But the Secret sits in the middle and knows!

The Last Word

The world is not conclusion:
A sequel stands beyond,
Invisible as music,
But positive as sound.
—EMILY DICKINSON

I T I S N O W more than two years since Hank walked out; and, in a strange way, I am still living, still resolving the story of my separation and its aftermath. In this time I have thought of, wanted, fantasied the full gamut from a resumption of the marriage to the finality of divorce.

Do not be deceived by my quiet, level tone of voice. Two years ago, I could not have commanded this clarity, this detachment. When it happened, I found separation unspeakable—literally locked within me. For relief, I filled notebooks with the record of my incredulity, pain, and panic—the inevitable fallout of separation. I recorded the details of happenings, meetings, conversations, as they took place. And I held an unending interview with myself. A kind of archeological "dig" in the mind, which brought up a seemingly limitless supply of buried artifacts about my marriage, my self, and—unexpectedly—the equally complex marriages from which Hank and I had issued.

While I found my relief in filling several dime-store notebooks, I soon discovered that I was expected to talk! Women patently unhappy in their own marriages came to ask: "How do you handle the loneliness?"—to seek, I suspected, their own last straw in determining whether to stay or to go. A man in bed with me wanted to know: "How's your sex life?" Most challenging were the questions Hank asked when I saw him for the first time after separation. "What did you tell yourself? How did you explain it?" he asked me.

And so grew the idea for this telling.

I am surprised, intrigued, and in some ways disappointed with what I have written here. At first, I could hardly force myself to return to the raw emotions of the early separation. The past could all too easily stir up a welter of bits and pieces and make me once again the un-put-together parts of a jigsaw puzzle. When I invited my mind, my feelings, my memories, the words took their own course—like a spring stream forcing a new channel of passage.

I intended to cite the theories and observations of marriage experts. But I found, to my chagrin, that one authority flatly contradicted another, equally authoritative, expert—to the point of chaos. I could not fit myself into any one pattern without cutting and chipping away at parts of me— those parts that define my individuality, and which are indivisible from the whole. I simply elbowed my way past sociology and theory to my own solution—if it *is* a solution.

I have arrived at no great truths of my own, no magnificent revelations about marriage in general, no advice I would *dare* pass on to another woman contemplating separation. I found only bits and pieces that pass for wisdom because they seem to work for me, today.

What *is* different is what I tell myself.

I tell myself, two years later, that judgment of my marriage is no longer obsessively important. That the judgment is made of words. Not tears. Not even truths that remain truths for more than a moment. My marriage to Hank *was* a marriage. It did exist. And each marriage, like each individual life, is its own story, opaque with dilemma.

I tell myself I am going back to Hank more of a woman, not less, even though I am older and presumably more obsolescent. I know there is a Madame Bovary in me, restless and discontent, a vestigial adolescent dreaming of a prince. But there is also a "good woman," sturdy and reliable; she is the "good girl" grown up. There's the child, too, who cannot escape the eternity of her childhood, who seeks solace in a mystical union with open space, sky, and grass. I am all of these returning to the marriage, eager not to be lost in routines, still shopping for moments of ecstasy, still desiring to be in passionate intercourse with life.

All along, I knew Hank's moods and weaknesses intimately—and dwelt on them; but now I know that *I* am searching for certainty where none exists, waving about my principles, while I am pragmatic—even venal; that I fancy myself generous—until I face the risk that there may be less for me. Above all, I know I am glad to be sheltered by Hank, with whatever warmth and support he offers me.

I do not agree with Lenore Coleman, the woman lawyer, who contends that affection runs downhill. I believe it ebbs and flows, as do respect, pleasure, sex, ease, and good fortune! Not the stuff of romantics so much as the stuff of living and learning.

I tell myself that Hank and I can offer each other affection, effort, and the knowledge that in the harsh world of present and future shock, we have more together than apart; that

> . . . we need the tether
> Of entering each other's lives, eyes
> wide apart, crying.*

It is impossible as I write today to ignore the women's liberation movement and the freedom within or without a marriage for which it is fighting. Against this background, I know that I did not behave like, did not feel like, a "free" woman during my separation. I accepted responsibility for myself only because I had no choice. I used my sex willfully and knowingly; my only regret, that I did not have the fresh, unmarred equipment of many years before. I would most certainly have used it!

And now I am returning to a marriage that looks "old-fashioned" and has obligations I know will not always allow me to do, even to say, what I wish. In making my choice, I have bartered away what looks like a portion of my freedom. But I have my own reactions to freedom, which is the current "gold standard" of our emotions, successor to previous standards of "adjustment" and "maturity." I did not find freedom intoxicating—at least, not for long. I found it a vast desert in which I was lost—without a compass.

I do, however, still have my private struggle to be free. I do not need to be freed from responsibilities and relationships, but from my own angers, crossed wires, crossed purposes. I want to be free to have a self: a self I can love and cherish.

It is the small, small beginnings of *this* freedom that I

* "Parergon," by John Ashbury. Reprinted from the *Columbia University Forum*.

have wrested from the tears and the adventures of these past two years. "With a great price, bought I this freedom." And even now, I can never be certain that it is mine for more than moments at a time, great exhilarating moments when the world becomes brilliant in hue, vibrating in every tree and stone and person with Being.

What will happen to this knowledge, to the new things I tell myself, to the moments I can soar, when I go back into everyday life with Hank? I will not open the door to a Lady or a Tiger. Nothing so dramatic or drastic. The future, like the past, is far more likely to go slowly, inconclusively through the revolving door of the soap opera.

And so I cannot write an ending. If I do not pretend to know what will come next, it is partly out of humility, partly out of superstition. I dare not anger the gods by predicting that things *will* be better. I know that my life and Hank's, like the long natural novel of our lives, will continue to write themselves; that I will turn the pages, my own reader, to choices and nonchoices, and to many endings before the only ending there is.